M000106640

25 Prewriting Graphic Organizers & Planning Sheets

by Jane Roberts

Must-Have Tools to Help All Students Gather and Organize Their Thoughts to Jumpstart the Writing Process

New York • Toronto • London • Auckland • Sydney
New Delhi • Mexico City • Hong Kong • Buenos Aires

Teaching *Resources*

Cover design by Reliable Design Studios
Interior design by NEO Grafika

ISBN 0-439-51369-3
Copyright © 2004 by Jane M.E. Roberts
All rights reserved.
Printed in the U.S.A.

1 2 3 4 5 6 7 8 9 10   40   11 10 09 08 07 06 05 04

Table of Contents

Introduction

Imagine your students during a writing lesson. Some are working in pairs, earnestly discussing their topic and using an acrostic-type planning sheet to list strong vocabulary words for their story. In one corner a student rifles through file folders filled with various graphic organizers, chooses one, and starts mapping out her story. In another part of the classroom, a small group of students is role-playing, acting out their story and jotting down notes about their characters.

Writing can be such an exciting adventure for students when they have a firm idea of what to write about and how to get started. The prewriting stage of the writing process (which also includes drafting, revising, editing, and publishing) is the place to build students' confidence and enthusiasm. Prewriting is like a rehearsal, a sketch, a conversation, a fleeting notion, or an earnest endeavor to produce a written outline.

Inside this book, you'll find 25 reproducible prewriting frameworks—planning sheets and graphic organizers—to help your students get started, along with sample lesson plans to help you become more comfortable teaching this aspect of writing. Once you've familiarized students with the variety of prewriting frameworks in this book, you can stand back and watch their motivation and enthusiasm soar. Students who use prewriting frameworks are more than eager to write, knowing that they can use them to generate and organize their ideas. This book is sure to make prewriting a positive experience for you and your students.

Enjoy!

Prewriting

The First Stage of the Writing Process

In this chapter, I will define prewriting, discuss its importance with particular reference to standards, and outline planning for prewriting.

What Is Prewriting?

Before students begin the first draft of a writing assignment, they should engage in a prewriting activity. Prewriting helps students create images and ideas about the assigned topic, as well as consider their emotions and values in relation to the topic. It involves recalling, finding, analyzing, and organizing content. Prewriting may also include listening to music, moving around the room, dramatizing scenes, looking at or drawing pictures—all behaviors to help students think about a topic. For example, picture Eileen writing in her corner, alone with her story map. At the same time, David and Jeff leaf through some books on the solar system, talking and jotting notes as they compare and contrast Jupiter and Saturn. Rita sketches and labels what she knows about an Iroquois longhouse, while Miguel crouches under a table, wearing headphones as he develops a web about his favorite composer.

While it can involve a variety of activities, prewriting by definition must include writing. Students should save their prewriting work and refer to it during subsequent stages of the writing process. Your students' prewriting will be messy. It may look like a list, a web, a checkerboard, a cartoon, or a storyboard. There will be arrows, words that have been crossed out, question marks and notes in the margin. Prewriting is whatever series of activities it takes to get your students to the point where they are eager to begin the actual draft.

Prewriting frameworks—planning sheets and graphic organizers—help students get ready to write the actual first draft. The 25 frameworks and 14 lessons in this book provide a good basis for teaching prewriting in your classes.

Why Focus on Prewriting?

As you plan writing activities for your class, always keep in mind that: (1) children do not write like adults, and (2) research shows that achievement is higher when students use prewriting strategies.

Children Do Not Write Like Adults

Here are some ways experienced writers tackle a writing project, and how children differ:
- Experienced writers plan their work carefully. Left on their own, children will do very little planning.
- A novelist may spend six months developing characters and plot, a year writing the first draft, and six months revising her manuscript. A child hopes that the story will unfold itself on paper.

- Experienced writers claim to discover new ideas while writing. Most children write what they already know.
- Experienced writers are reluctant to tell their story before it is written. Children want to discuss their ideas before they write.
- Adults focus more on the content than on the mechanics, and craft their work during revision. Children do not have the knowledge or experience of older writers, and many struggle with vocabulary and mechanics.

Given these dramatic differences between children and adults, you can see how important it is to give students a basis in prewriting to make their final drafts more effective. Students gain experience through instruction, using prewriting frameworks to plan their work and talk about their ideas so that they are eager to write.

Achievement Is Higher When Students Use Prewriting Strategies

Students who feel unsuccessful in writing may experience resistance, frustration, and fear during prewriting. They may turn to the physical escapes of sharpening pencils or going to the bathroom, and may even blank out on words. As one researcher explains, "Poorer writers tend to spend little time planning, rushing to commit words to the page, and to hold tight to their initial formulations of a problem" (Hull, 1989, p. 107, referring to studies by Flowers and Hayes).

In a study of unskilled writers, Sondra Perl (1979, p. 328) found that the average time spent on prewriting was four minutes, and that three prewriting strategies were used:

1. Rephrasing the topic until a particular word or idea connected with the student's experience. Then the student had an "event" in mind before writing began.

2. Turning the large conceptual issue in the topic (e.g., equality) into two manageable pieces of writing (e.g., rich vs. poor; black vs. white).

3. Initiating a string of associations to a word in the topic and then developing one or more of those associations during writing.

In this particular study, while students using the above strategies began to write with an idea of what they wanted to say, most students, after reading the prompt two or three times, "had no idea what to write…acknowledging only that they would figure it out as they went along" (Perl, 1979).

In contrast, more successful students experience prewriting as curiosity leading to confidence. As teachers, we want to give our students this confidence in their ability to write.

Students are most successful when they have talked through their ideas; when they know how to begin, elaborate, and end; when they have a vocabulary bank and a clear understanding of the content. If students have clear assignment guidelines, they feel less anxious. If they use prewriting planning sheets and graphic organizers well, they are more confident. If, like experienced writers, they spend up to 25 percent of their allocated assignment time on prewriting, their level of success increases a great deal. Effective prewriting gives students the vocabulary, focus, content, and organization needed to complete the assignment successfully.

Prewriting strategies are not innate abilities; they are thinking skills that can be taught and learned. Students need direct instruction in developing and using prewriting frameworks so that they can apply them independently. A summary of research on effective practice in writing states "that students who are encouraged to engage in an array of prewriting experiences evidence greater writing achievement than those enjoined to 'get to work' on their writing without this kind of preparation" (Cotton, 1988).

Why Is Prewriting Important?

Prewriting is important because it is the stage at which students understand the assignment, when they begin to access the information they need, and when they become motivated to get started.

In the prewriting stage students clarify the assignment for themselves. They need to know the topic, purpose, and audience for the assignment. They need to tell themselves what they already know about the topic and what else they may need to find out. They need to ask themselves why and for whom they are writing. If they think about these questions, they will learn to write differently when planning a holiday story for a first grader, for example, than when writing game directions for their peers.

During prewriting, as students write vocabulary relevant to the topic, use phrases to capture recalled images, and answer questions posed by a framework, they acquire a bank of words from which to draw as they build the sentences that create the story. They also develop ways to organize their ideas. Since prewriting usually includes peer interaction, it offers students the opportunity to hitchhike on others' ideas and validate their own. Students become more motivated as they share their prewriting, increasing their belief that they can accomplish the assignment successfully.

Lucy Calkins states, "Our students need to postpone writing until their information begins to coalesce into ideas, and until they feel a sense of authority. Then they need to write" (1986, p. 284).

Prewriting in the Standards-Based Curriculum

Students' achievement is measured against standards. Achievement is higher in writing when prewriting strategies are used. Therefore, in planning standards-based curriculum and instruction, you need to pay attention to prewriting. Development of standards began in the early 1990s, and includes attention to types of writing and quality of writing.

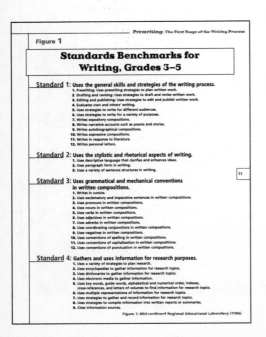

A Little History

Since the early 1990s national and state educational agencies have been developing standards. More recently tests addressing those standards have been administered to students in grades 3 and above. Writing tests often require students to hand in all their work, including prewriting. Teachers and students are held accountable to meet those standards.

In 1996 McREL (Mid-continent Regional Educational Laboratory), funded by the National Institute of Education, synthesized many sets of standards and benchmarks for writing in grades 3 through 5. (See Figure 1, page 11.)

Examples of Standards for Writing Quality

In Pennsylvania, standards of writing quality are organized by domain: focus, content, organization, style, and conventions (i.e., grammar and mechanics). These five domains of writing are simply defined in Figure 2 (page 12), and in more detail in Figure 3 (page 13). I use the Pennsylvania standards as an example since they are comprehensive and similar to standards used in other states. In my examples of lesson plans, I also use the Pennsylvania domains. If you don't use domains already, you might find these helpful.

Some teachers may use fewer domains or categories for writing. For instance, a common division is content versus mechanics. This division allows teachers to reward students who can strongly develop their ideas even if they have weak usage and mechanics. Comparing this simple division to Pennsylvania's writing domains, content includes focus, content, and organization, while mechanics covers style and conventions.

Teachers who use the 6+1 traits of writing will find it very similar to the domains I use. Both the Pennsylvania domains and the 6+1 traits cover organization and conventions. In the 6+1 traits, ideas cover the focus and content domains used in the Pennsylvania system. Also, while the Pennsylvania domains have a category for style, the 6+1 traits divide style into voice, word choice, and sentence fluency. Presentation in the 6+1 model is covered in the conventions category for the Pennsylvania model. If you use other writing domains or traits, you will probably see similarities as well. Your experience will help you adjust the ideas to fit your needs.

In state tests, Pennsylvania students' writing is assessed equally across the five domains, yet traditionally teachers of younger students have paid more attention to the conventions than to the other four domains. All domains can be addressed more easily if prewriting frameworks are used. Therefore, using prewriting frameworks should help students perform better on standardized tests.

Examples of Standards for Types of Writing

In most states, types of writing include narrative, informative, and persuasive. Figure 4 (page 14) defines these types of writing. Since writing across the curriculum is also tested, teachers need to look at the types of writing required in other subjects. Analysis of standards for Pennsylvania's 3rd and 6th grades in science, social studies, and reading identifies additional types and topics for writing. (See Figures 5 and 6, pages 15 and 16.) Test prompts require students to "identify and discuss," "explain," and "define and describe." Currently these types of prompts are not often used in 3rd grade, but they are used in later grades.

Figure 4
Standards for Types of Writing, Grades 3 and 5

Grade 3: Standard 1.4.3
A. Write narrative pieces (e.g., stories, poems, plays).
 • Include detailed descriptions of people, places, and things
 • Use relevant illustrations
 • Include literary elements
B. Write informational pieces (descriptions, letters, reports, instructions) using illustrations when relevant.
C. Write...

Figure 3
Standards for Types of Writing, Grades 3 and 5

Grade 3: Standard 1.5.3
A. Write with a sharp, distinct focus identifying topic, task, and audience.
B. Write using well-developed content appropriate for the topic.

Grade 5: Standard 1.5.5
A. Write with a sharp, distinct focus identifying topic, task, and audience.
B. Write using well-developed content

Figure 2
Simple Definitions of the Five Domains of Writing

Focus
 • What is this about?
 • Did I stick to the topic?

Content
 • Are there facts, details, examples, or explanations?
 • Is it interesting?

Organization
 • Are ideas grouped in a sensible way?
 • Is information in the right order?
 • Is there a clear beginning, middle, and end?

Style
 • Does the kind of writing fit the topic?
 • Are the sentences varied?
 • Are there clear word pictures and strong vocabulary?

Conventions
 • Does it have correct spelling, punctuation, capitalization, word use, and paragraphing?
 • Is it easy to read?

Figure 6
Examples of Types and Topics of Writing for Sixth Grade

Types of Writing

Figure 5
Examples of Types and Topics of Writing for Third Grade

Types of Writing

Narrative
 • Stories
 • Poems
 • Plays

Informational
 • Descriptions
 • Letters
 • Reports
 • Instructions
 • Directions

Persuasive
 • Opinions supported by facts

Definitions of processes or systems

Explanations

Questions

Comparisons

Summaries

Topics for Writing
 • Animals
 • Plants
 • Elements of survival for living things
 • Processes, e.g., erosion
 • States of matter
 • Simple machines
 • Seasons
 • Weather, evaporation and condensation
 • Measurement and related tools
 • Environments/habitats
 • Map skills, land forms

 • Climate, environment, resources: impact on how people live
 • Goods and services, trade and barter
 • Rules, laws, and government
 • U.S symbols
 • U.S. Constitution
 • Taxes
 • Important individuals and groups: state, U.S., world
 • Historical evidence
 • Early and recent civilizations
 • Personal experience
 • Literature

9

Planning for Prewriting

When planning a writing assignment, you need to plan for every stage. Ask yourself what students already know and what they will need to know to help you decide if you need to start some prewriting activities even before you give students the actual writing assignment. For instance, if your students are going to write about erosion caused by water, they will need to understand the process of erosion and they will need appropriate vocabulary. During social studies and science lessons, you might structure note-taking so that students have relevant information. In the same week your students may develop lists of verbs (present, past, future) about the movement of water (e.g., *splash, swirl, ripple*) as part of a language-arts activity. Later that week give the assignment: *Write about a sand castle or dam that you built, and the successes and challenges of working against the force of tide and/or current*. Your students will already have some notes and lists that become part of their prewriting.

After you give the assignment, your students' first step of prewriting is to analyze the writing prompt or guidelines given (Pritchard, 1994). Students must understand the nature and scope of the topic, the audience and purpose, and the best organizational strategy for this assignment.

Nowadays most teachers try to give carefully crafted prompts. They do not tell the students to write an essay on birds; they write the prompt on the board: *Describe the general characteristics of birds, with two or three examples, for a class report*. While most 3rd or 4th graders would say that they understand the assignment, some would admit that they aren't sure what "characteristics" mean, and a few would be wondering whether the choice of illustrative examples had to relate somehow to the characteristics discussed.

Some teachers clarify an assignment by listing the domains of writing quality and establishing standards criteria for those domains. For younger students, the teacher may simply post the criteria with the assignment prompt. Older students derive the criteria by analyzing the prompt. For example, standards criteria for the prompt about birds could be:

Focus: characteristics of birds, class report

Content: two or three examples

Organization: introduction, topic paragraphs, conclusion

Style: content-specific vocabulary, clear explanations

Conventions: spelling, punctuation, paragraphs

If you establish an expectation that students need to ask themselves and each other about the exact meaning of the assignment, the questioning will be comfortable and helpful, with some answers coming from you and some from other students. Since analysis of the assignment is part of prewriting, students should write their understanding of the task. Standards criteria clarify the writing task, help to guide revision, and may be used for assessment.

The second step in prewriting is gathering and organizing information. Too often teachers suggest brainstorming, helping students come up with some ideas before they move on to the drafting stage. There are many strategies besides brainstorming for gathering and organizing ideas. This book describes 25 of those strategies in the form of prewriting planning sheets and graphic organizers and shows how they can be used.

Offer students a variety of prewriting frameworks, and help develop their ability to use appropriate ones independently. The lessons in this book are designed to give you a basis in using different planning sheets and graphic organizers. Good luck with this exciting part of the writing process!

Figure 1

Standards Benchmarks for Writing, Grades 3–5

Standard 1: Uses the general skills and strategies of the writing process.
1. Prewriting: Uses prewriting strategies to plan written work.
2. Drafting and revising: Uses strategies to draft and revise written work.
3. Editing and publishing: Uses strategies to edit and publish written work.
4. Evaluates own and others' writing.
5. Uses strategies to write for different audiences.
6. Uses strategies to write for a variety of purposes.
7. Writes expository compositions.
8. Writes narrative accounts such as poems and stories.
9. Writes autobiographical compositions.
10. Writes expressive compositions.
11. Writes in response to literature.
12. Writes personal letters.

Standard 2: Uses the stylistic and rhetorical aspects of writing.
1. Uses descriptive language that clarifies and enhances ideas.
2. Uses paragraph form in writing.
3. Uses a variety of sentence structures in writing.

Standard 3: Uses grammatical and mechanical conventions in written compositions.
1. Writes in cursive.
2. Uses exclamatory and imperative sentences in written compositions.
3. Uses pronouns in written compositions.
4. Uses nouns in written compositions.
5. Uses verbs in written compositions.
6. Uses adjectives in written compositions.
7. Uses adverbs in written compositions.
8. Uses coordinating conjunctions in written compositions.
9. Uses negatives in written compositions.
10. Uses conventions of spelling in written compositions.
11. Uses conventions of capitalization in written compositions.
12. Uses conventions of punctuation in written compositions.

Standard 4: Gathers and uses information for research purposes.
1. Uses a variety of strategies to plan research.
2. Uses encyclopedias to gather information for research topics.
3. Uses dictionaries to gather information for research topics.
4. Uses electronic media to gather information.
5. Uses key words, guide words, alphabetical and numerical order, indexes, cross-references, and letters of volumes to find information for research topics.
6. Uses multiple representations of information for research topics.
7. Uses strategies to gather and record information for research topics.
8. Uses strategies to compile information into written reports or summaries.
9. Cites information sources.

Figure 1: Mid-continent Regional Educational Laboratory (1996)

11

Figure 2

Simple Definitions of the Five Domains of Writing

Focus

- What is this about?
- Did I stick to the topic?

Content

- Are there facts, details, examples, or explanations?
- Is it interesting?

Organization

- Are ideas grouped in a sensible way?
- Is information in the right order?
- Is there a clear beginning, middle, and end?

Style

- Does the kind of writing fit the topic?
- Are the sentences varied?
- Are there clear word pictures and strong vocabulary?

Conventions

- Does it have correct spelling, punctuation, capitalization, word use, and paragraphing?
- Is it easy to read?

Figure 3

Standards for Types of Writing, Grades 3 and 5

Grade 3: Standard 1.5.3

A. Write with a sharp, distinct focus identifying topic, task, and audience.

B. Write using well-developed content appropriate for the topic.
- Gather and organize information.
- Write a series of related sentences or paragraphs with one central idea.
- Incorporate details relevant and appropriate to the topic.

C. Write with controlled and/or subtle organization.
- Sustain a logical order.
- Include a recognizable beginning, middle, and end.

D. Write with an awareness of the stylistic aspects of composition.
- Use sentences of differing lengths and complexities.
- Use descriptive words and action verbs.

E. Revise writing to improve detail and order by identifying missing information and determining whether ideas follow logically.

F. Edit writing using the conventions of language.
- Spell common, frequently used words correctly.
- Use capital letters correctly (first word in sentences, proper nouns, pronoun "I").
- Punctuate correctly (periods, exclamation points, question marks, commas in a series).
- Use nouns, pronouns, verbs, adjectives, adverbs and conjunctions properly.
- Use complete sentences (simple, compound, declarative, interrogative, exclamatory and imperative).

G. Present and/or defend written work for publication when appropriate.

Grade 5: Standard 1.5.5

A. Write with a sharp, distinct focus identifying topic, task, and audience.

B. Write using well-developed content appropriate for the topic.
- Gather, organize and select the most effective information appropriate for the topic, task, and audience.
- Write paragraphs that have a topic sentence and supporting details.

C. Write with controlled and/or subtle organization.
- Sustain a logical order within sentences and between paragraphs, using meaningful transitions.
- Include an identifiable introduction, body, and conclusion.

D. Write with an understanding of the stylistic aspects of composition.
- Use different types and lengths of sentences.
- Use precise language including adjectives, adverbs, action verbs and specific details that convey the writer's meaning.
- Develop and maintain a consistent voice.

E. Revise writing to improve organization and word choice; check the logic, order of ideas and precision of vocabulary.

F. Edit writing using the conventions of language.
- Spell common, frequently used words correctly.
- Use capital letters correctly.
- Punctuate correctly (periods, exclamation points, question marks, commas, quotation marks, apostrophes).
- Use nouns, pronouns, verbs, adjectives, adverbs, conjunctions, prepositions and interjections properly.
- Use complete sentences (simple, compound, declarative, interrogative, exclamatory and imperative).

G. Present and/or defend written work for publication when appropriate.

13

Figure 3: Pennsylvania Department of Education

Figure 4

Standards for Types of Writing, Grades 3 and 5

Grade 3: Standard 1.4.3

A. Write narrative pieces
(e.g., stories, poems, plays).
   - Include detailed descriptions of people, places, and things.
   - Use relevant illustrations.
   - Include literary elements.

B. Write informational pieces (e.g., descriptions, letters, reports, instructions) using illustrations when relevant.

C. Write an opinion and support it with facts.

Grade 5: Standard 1.4.5

A. Write poems, plays, and multi-paragraph stories.
   - Include detailed descriptions of people, places, and things.
   - Use relevant illustrations.
   - Include literary elements.
   - Utilize dialog.
   - Apply literary conflict.
   - Use literary devices.

B. Write multi-paragraph informational pieces (e.g., essays, descriptions, letters, reports, instructions).
   - Include cause and effect.
   - Develop a problem and solution when appropriate to the topic.
   - Use relevant graphics (e.g., maps, charts, graphs, tables, illustrations, photographs).

C. Write persuasive pieces with a clearly stated position or opinion and supporting detail, citing sources when needed.

14

Figure 4: Pennsylvania Department of Education

Figure 5

Examples of Types and Topics of Writing for Third Grade

Types of Writing

Narrative
- Stories
- Poems
- Plays

Informational
- Descriptions
- Letters
- Reports
- Instructions
- Directions

Persuasive
- Opinions supported by facts

Definitions of processes or systems

Explanations

Questions

Comparisons

Summaries

Topics for Writing

- Animals
- Plants
- Elements of survival for living things
- Processes, e.g., erosion
- States of matter
- Simple machines
- Seasons
- Weather, evaporation and condensation
- Measurement and related tools
- Environments/habitats
- Map skills, land forms

- Climate, environment, resources: impact on how people live
- Goods and services, trade and barter
- Rules, laws, and government
- U.S symbols
- U.S. Constitution
- Taxes
- Important individuals and groups: state, U.S., world
- Historical evidence
- Early and recent civilizations
- Personal experience
- Literature

15

Figure 6

Examples of Types and Topics of Writing for Sixth Grade

Types of Writing

Narrative
- Stories
- Poems
- Plays

Informational
- Descriptions
- Letters
- Reports
- Instructions
- Directions
- Articles
- Interviews

Persuasive
- Opinions supported by facts

Definitions of processes or systems

Explanations

Questions

Comparisons

Summaries

Topics for Writing

- Principles of government
- Purpose and symbols of holidays
- Principles and ideals found in famous historical speeches
- Rights and responsibilities of U.S. citizens
- Consequences of following or violating rules
- State history to the mid-1800s
- Early inhabitants of the state: lifestyles, conflict, cooperation
- State agriculture, trade, and transportation to mid-1800s
- U.S. leaders to 1824
- Famous U.S. historic sites and documents

- Conflict and cooperation among U.S. groups to 1824
- Cultural and political contributions by famous people in Asia, Africa, Europe, and the Americas
- Climate
- Geographical regions: physical, cultural, political and economic characteristics
- Interaction between people and the environment
- Systems: natural and physical
- Energy sources and uses
- Solar system
- Environment and use of resources
- Technology and society

Overview of 25 Prewriting Frameworks

So far in this book, I've discussed the importance of prewriting. In this chapter, I will briefly describe 25 prewriting frameworks—planning sheets and graphic organizers—in alphabetical order for easy reference. Thumbnail pictures help you see how students might use the frameworks. Note that these planning sheets and graphic organizers are not mutually exclusive: two or more may be used for the same assignment. You will find reproducible pages of the planning sheets and graphic organizers in Chapter 5, starting on page 70.

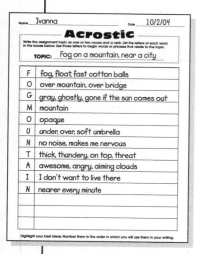

1. ACROSTIC

Students use this planning sheet to build a bank of words and phrases, somewhat like a semi-structured brainstorming. It is useful for topics familiar to students and for topics easily visualized (e.g. cleaning my room, riding the school bus).

Ask students to define the writing topic using one or two nouns and a verb. Then have them write the letters of the words, each letter on a line by itself, going down the page. Invite students to use those first letters to begin words or phrases that relate to the topic. When they have worked for 5 to 10 minutes, alone or in pairs, have them share their words or phrases in small groups, and then with the class. Encourage students to hitchhike on others' ideas. To move students into the drafting stage, ask them to highlight and sequence the ideas they like best.

2. BRAINSTORM

Students quickly generate random ideas and words with this planning sheet. It is useful to get a quick start, with students recalling or using free association on a given topic. The more unfamiliar the topic, the more you will need to cue students and encourage hitchhiking in groups or with the whole class.

Ask students to write the topic at the top of the page. For about two minutes, allow students to jot down anything that comes to mind about the topic. Tell them not to criticize themselves. Each time students stop, they write "Zzz…" Cue them with questions, such as

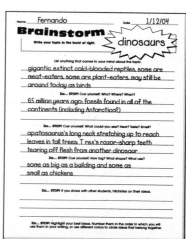

who; where; and what does it look, sound, taste, and feel like? What is its size, shape, and color? Have students share their ideas with a partner or with the class and add to their notes. After reviewing the assignment guidelines, have students highlight their best ideas and group them to help organize their writing.

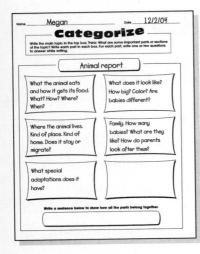

3. CATEGORIZE

This graphic organizer is useful for research projects because it breaks a large topic into manageable sections. It helps students analyze a topic, then organize their ideas.

Have students read an assigned writing prompt carefully to see if it suggests categories or sections that should be included. If the assignment is more open-ended, such as writing about a state, an animal, or the solar system, refer students to books that show how the sections are organized, or have them work in groups to generate questions that will become their sections or categories. For instance, if students describe a country, they could divide it into regions, then each region by type of landform, climate, resources, or population density. You may ask students to define a category by a title, question, or topic sentence.

4. CAUSE AND EFFECT

Use this graphic organizer to identify causes leading to an effect. Students will find this useful when they have to explain a process or event in science or social studies.

Have students begin with the effect, noting it at the top of the page. Ask, *"What happened immediately before to cause this effect?"* Sometimes there will be a chain of causes, occurring one after another. Sometimes several causes happen together to bring about a single effect. Have students write one cause in each box. When students have noted all the causes, ask them to draw connecting arrows between the boxes and to the effect to show the sequence or simultaneous action. After making brief notes about each cause, have students decide how to put the causes in order to explain the process clearly.

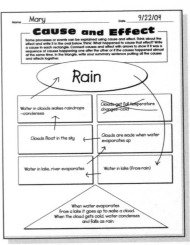

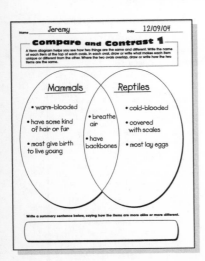

5. COMPARE AND CONTRAST

There are two graphic organizers that are useful to compare and contrast topics:

(1) A Venn diagram (two overlapping circles) notes similarities and differences between two things through words or pictures. Because ideas are randomly generated, this graphic organizer is useful for younger students or for students unfamiliar with comparing and contrasting. Have students label each circle with a topic. Explain that the outer separate sections are for describing characteristics unique to each item, while the central overlapping section is for characteristics common to both items. Have students make notes or draw little pictures. When finished, invite students to write a sentence describing how the two items are more alike or more different. This sentence becomes the thesis of their written work.

(2) The second graphic organizer, a four-column chart, requires higher-order critical-thinking skills, and is useful for more complex topics. Have students begin by generating categories or questions that will be listed in the first column. (For instance, if comparing trees, students might list: size, shape, type, bark, leaves, flower/seed/fruit, use.) Have students use columns 2 and 4 to name the items being compared, and to answer the questions on each row, noting each item's unique characteristics. Use column 3 to note characteristics that are common to both items. Students then write a summary sentence, or thesis statement, highlighting key differences and/or similarities between the two objects.

6. CONTEXT ANALYSIS

This planning sheet, useful in social studies, science, and literature, analyzes a situation, issue, or environment. It helps students clarify their understanding of an issue, as they make notes in response to five questions. Students may then use those notes to write an essay following the structure of the framework. Or they may break answers for each question into sections to be addressed by a research project.

Begin by having students note the issue (e.g., pollution of the Great Lakes, school athletics program). Encourage them to work alone or with a partner to answer these questions:

1) What are its characteristics?
2) How has it changed over time?
3) How is it part of something else?
4) How does it influence other things or people?
5) Why is it important?

(Adapted from Pritchard, 1994)

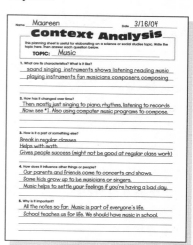

7. DRAW

Perfect for visual learners, this graphic organizer illustrates the beginning, middle, and end of a situation. It helps students visualize a personal experience or historical event and sequence what happened. Students can also use this organizer to plan a creative story. Since it focuses on three important scenes and invites detailed writing, this organizer helps students avoid the routine "bed-to-bed" stories.

Invite students to begin with the middle panel and sketch a scene or character in a critical situation. Have students write a speech bubble for the character(s) or write a descriptive sentence below the drawing. Ask students to consider what led to that situation and sketch it in the beginning panel. Then have students determine the ending or resolution, sketching it in the third panel. Encourage students to expand and connect their sentences and to narrate the event in detail. After writing their final draft, students can use their sketches as reference for final illustrations.

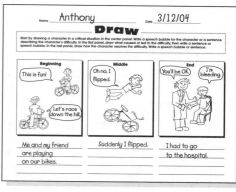

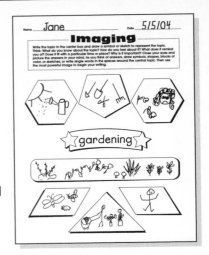

8. IMAGING

This graphic organizer has two forms, both of which ask students to create mental images:

(1) The first form of imaging invites visual free association. It is useful for dealing with emotionally charged topics or abstract ideas, to write poetry or strong descriptive paragraphs. It is most successful when students use color. Have students represent the topic with a symbol or sketch in the middle of the page, and then add symbols or words around the central image to show: a) what they know; b) what they associate with this; c) what feelings or ideas they have about this; and d) why it is important. Have students begin their writing with the most powerful image. (Adapted from Pritchard, 1994)

(2) The second form of imaging is purposeful and personal. (Professional athletes do this just before a competition.) It is useful when students have to explain an activity. Ask students to think of an activity (e.g., conducting a science experiment, making a sandwich, shooting a basket). Invite them to close their eyes and imagine themselves doing the activity. Tell them to think of the environment and objects involved, make a series of images for the sequence of activities, and feel themselves carrying it out. When students understand the concept of imaging, have them repeat the exercise, stopping to make lists of items needed for the activity and writing sequential notes to capture the images with strong vocabulary.

9. INTERVIEW

Encourage students to use this planning sheet to help come up with questions to conduct interviews. It helps students organize their ideas, recall what they know, and decide what they need to know.

Have students begin with linking questions: Who? What? Where? When? How? Why? They may also consider the questions in **Context Analysis** if the topic is appropriate. If you are giving a structured assignment, have students determine the important parts and make up appropriate questions. Encourage them to consider what they already know about this topic and make up questions that would bring out interesting details. Finally, tell students that they should include at least one open-ended question to allow the person they're interviewing to tell something he or she thinks is especially important about the topic.

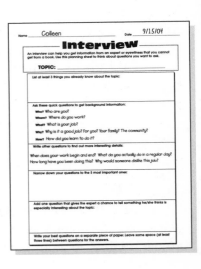

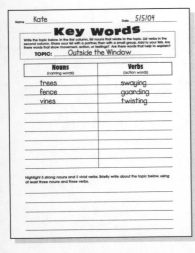

10. KEY WORDS

This graphic organizer is helpful for generating a word bank of nouns and verbs. More structured than **Brainstorming**, it is useful for almost all assignments, but particularly when you are encouraging use of strong vocabulary.

Have students write the topic at the top of the page. Then challenge them to list all the relevant nouns and verbs they can think of in one minute. Encourage students to share their lists with a partner and add to the lists. After another minute or two, have students share with a small group and add to the lists. (I use big laminated poster boards and washable markers so that groups can share their lists.) Review responses with the class, listing some strong examples on the board. Are there words that relate to each of the senses, words that show movement, action, and emotion? Have students add to the lists. Then ask each student to highlight five vivid verbs and five strong nouns and use them in sentences for their writing assignment.

11. KEY WORDS EXTENDED

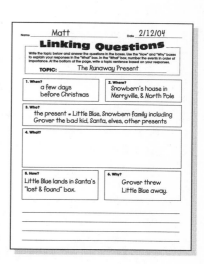

By adding adjectives and adverbs to **Key Words**, this graphic organizer helps students recognize and use these parts of speech and encourages varied vocabulary and sentence construction.

For practice, invite the class to work with you as you write some examples on the board (e.g., *serious, penguin, slipped, suddenly*). Ask volunteers to make up sentences using sets of words. You might also show them different forms of the same base word, such as *excite, exciting, excitement, excitedly.*

When students are ready to work on their own, ask them to write the topic at the top of the page. Have them list words in the labeled columns: Adjectives, Nouns, Verbs, and Adverbs. After hitchhiking ideas from classmates, students should highlight 10 to 20 words they will use in their writing and draft one or two sentences using those words.

12. LINKING QUESTIONS

This graphic organizer uses traditional structuring questions to help students identify the key elements of an assignment.

List the linking questions on the board and explain to students that news reporters frequently use these questions to structure their articles. Have students write the assignment (or topic) at the top of the page. Encourage students to answer the "When," "Where," and "Who" questions first. Explain that "What" often means "What happened?" Have students answer that question with a brief phrase. They should then answer "How" and "Why." Their answers to these two questions will probably explain "What." Invite students to use their notes to write a topic sentence that could introduce the writing (e.g., *One afternoon last summer my family and I were at Dewey Beach when something amazing happened.*) Have students go back to the "What" question to add details, then number the critical events described in sequence.

13. MAKE NOTES

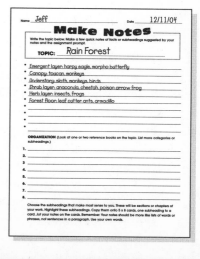

Students can use this planning sheet to build a knowledge base and begin to organize that knowledge. It is useful for work requiring analysis and synthesis, and for major assignments such as science or social studies projects.

Have students write the topic or focus of the assignment, and list a few quick notes of what they know about the topic. Encourage them to share their notes and review the assignment prompt to see if they could add categories or subtopics. After they have shared their notes, have students look at reference books on the topic for more ideas on subtopics or categories. Have students list subtopics selected from their quick notes under "Organization." Then have students write each subheading on a 5 x 8 note card. Allow time for students to conduct research and make notes. Remind them that notes do not have to be complete sentences and can include sketches. Notes are also easier to read if they look like lists rather than paragraphs.

14. OUTLINE

Perfect for older students, this planning sheet uses a traditional structure to organize ideas. It is useful as an extension of **Categorize**, and/or **Make Notes**. Before asking students to use this sheet as a prewriting strategy, help them understand outlining by using it to analyze a section of a textbook or a piece of their own writing.

Have students break the main topic into subtopics, using appropriate categories or a time line. Then ask students to break each subtopic into smaller sections. Use a numbering system (e.g., numbers for subtopics, lowercase letters for sections, and lowercase Roman numerals for subsections). For more sophisticated students, explain parallel values of levels within the outline.

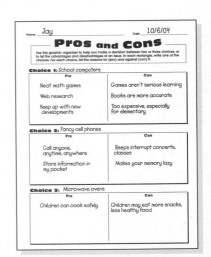

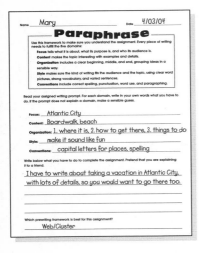

15. PARAPHRASE

This planning sheet helps students analyze a writing prompt or assignment guidelines, and is especially useful in test situations or if students are trying to define their own self-designed projects. Students can then determine exactly what they are required to do.

Have students recall, define, and list the five domains of writing (see page 12). Refer students to the assignment prompt to identify and write what they need to do for each domain. If the prompt does not state criteria for a particular domain, encourage students to make a sensible guess. Ask students to use their notes to summarize in their own words what they have to do. Encourage discussion to decide which other prewriting framework could be used to address that assignment.

16. PROS AND CONS

Help students identify advantages and disadvantages of decisions or choices using this simple graphic organizer. It is useful for generating ideas for a debate, examining both sides of an issue, or weighing the values of courses of action. It can be used in social studies, science, health, and literature.

Ask students to suggest alternate definitions of advantage and disadvantage, listing the vocabulary terms on the board (e.g., *good/bad*, *succeed/fail*, *for/against*). Present a realistic situation and lead a brief discussion to help students see that criteria such as personal and social values affect their perceptions of "good" or "bad." Assign the writing topic, asking students to identify the choice(s) inherent in that topic.

For each choice, challenge students to identify its advantages and disadvantages, making notes in the two columns. Students may then choose to present a balanced argument or use the notes to take one side over the other.

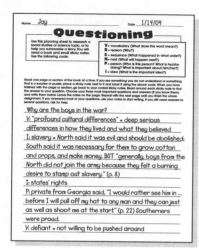

17. QUESTIONING

Similar to annotating, this planning sheet engages students in paraphrasing or summarizing, but does not invite them to write in a book. It structures comprehension of a section of social studies or science text or of a complex passage in fiction.

Refer students to two to four relevant pages of a book. Explain that good readers ask questions as they read. List and define the following question code:

V = vocabulary (What does this word mean?)

P = person (Who is this person? What is he/she doing? What's important about him/her?)

R = reason (Why?)

I = idea (What's the important idea?)

S = sequence (What happened in what order?)

N = next (What will happen next?)

Distribute small sticky notes to students. Explain that whenever questions come up as they read a passage, they should stick coded notes next to the passage. Tell students to read quickly through one page at a time. Have students work in pairs to discuss their questions. Then ask them to choose three to five important questions, put them in a sensible order, and write them on their prewriting sheet, leaving space for their answers. (Adapted from Keene & Zimmermann, 1997)

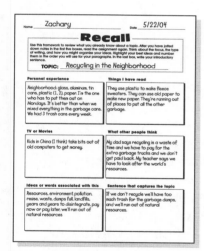

18. RECALL

This graphic organizer draws on students' memories. There are two versions:

(1) The first version includes cues and is useful for addressing current affairs. Ask students to write the topic. Have them consider and jot notes about the topic in five sections: a) personal experience; b) things I have read; c) TV or movies; d) what other people think or say about it; and e) associated words or ideas. Ask students to share their ideas with a partner, add ideas if they wish, and then write a sentence for the sixth section: capturing the topic. After considering the focus, type of writing, purpose, and audience, students should highlight their best ideas and number them for paragraph order.

(2) The second version of recall uses a "memory chain" to recall ideas. This is similar to a brainstorm list of single words or short groups of words, each word linked to the next one. It helps students identify or define specific elements of a personal experience. Explain the strategy to students, and engage the class in developing an example, using a shared experience, such as going on a field trip. Then have students choose their own topic and type of writing, using their personal experience as the basis. Ask students to write a memory chain, listing words or phrases down the page. After a few minutes, have them go back to their list, highlight the important topics, and, if they would find it useful, build additional chains from those important elements before drafting their writing.

19. ROLE-PLAY

Students work in small groups to act out a situation, then use this planning sheet to clarify characters and sequence of action. Kinesthetic learners will find this prewriting strategy very

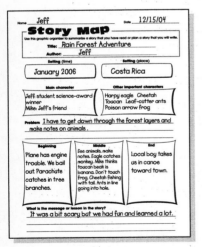

appealing. You may use this strategy to lead to story writing, narration of a historical incident, or script writing. (I use this planning sheet to introduce script writing, teaching this set of skills as students move into the drafting stage after prewriting.)

Tell students that they will be working in groups of three or four to plan a piece of writing that captures a scene. If you are giving a particular assignment (e.g., Washington's confrontation with the French in Pennsylvania, a commercial for a healthy snack, or a scene from literature), explain it to students first. Invite students to decide on characters (considering the actions, motives, and influences of the characters), setting, situation or problem, and resolution. As students make these decisions and record them on the planning sheet, they act out their ideas, improvising words and actions. Encourage students to revise their ideas as they rehearse them.

20. SKETCH AND LABEL

Popular with visual learners, this planning sheet requires students to sketch and label an object, system, or process. It helps students clarify an idea and organize how they will write about it.

Ask students to draw a rough diagram, map, or picture of the object or process that illustrates the assignment topic. Have them label important parts or steps and note the function or purpose of each. Encourage students to check their ideas with a partner. Finally, ask students to number the parts or steps in the order in which they will write about them.

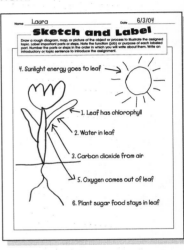

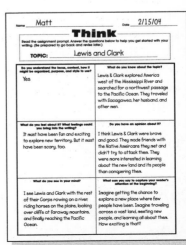

21. STORY MAP

This graphic organizer identifies the important components of a story. Students can use it to summarize a story that they have read, or to plan a story that they will write. (If summarizing, I have students work in groups using big laminated boards before they complete their own graphic organizers.)

Have students fill out the sections for characters, setting, problem, beginning, middle, end, resolution, and theme or message of the story. Before they write their rough drafts, have them review their responses with a partner or with you.

22. THINK

This prewriting activity provides little structure or assistance to students. You may want to use this to contrast for students the kinds of writing results they get by thinking from the results they get by using an appropriate framework. Too often, students left on their own rely only on thinking before jumping into writing the draft. Later, they end up having to do a great deal of revision.

Simply tell students to ask and answer for themselves what they know about the assigned topic, what they see and feel about it, and if they have an opinion about it. Have students begin writing when they are ready.

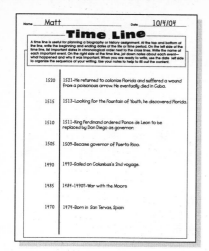

23. TIME LINE

Useful for planning a biography or history assignment, or for analyzing a series of events, this graphic organizer puts information in chronological order.

After identifying the topic, ask students to divide the time line into sections of equal value, noting dates or times. To the left of the line, have students write critical events next to their matching dates. To the right of the line, have students note the special features or significance of each event. The sequence to the left gives students a chronological organization. The notes to the right suggest themes, arguments, or points to be made.

24. WEB/CLUSTER

This graphic organizer identifies important elements of an event or story and the connections among those elements. Since it involves association of ideas, this graphic organizer can evoke a great deal of information and helps students group ideas.

Ask students to write the topic at the center of the page. Have them brainstorm or recall components of the topic or ideas associated with it, writing each idea in a separate oval, and connecting ovals to each other in related groups. Ask students to draw larger color-coded circles around groups and to number the circles in sequence for writing.

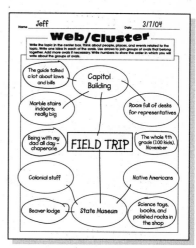

25. WRITE FREELY

Get students actively writing quickly with this strategy that invites unstructured writing. This planning sheet allows students to vent their feelings about a topic.

Tell students that after you give them the assignment or reveal the written prompt, they should begin to write freely—sentences, phrases, ideas, whatever comes to mind. Reveal the prompt, but do not discuss it. (The first time I introduce this strategy, I model it on the board as students write.) After five minutes, stop students. Ask them to read what they wrote, highlight interesting ideas or phrases, and review them with a partner. Then have students list at least two or three ideas that might help them organize their writing. Discuss the ideas with the class. Invite students to decide on a point of view, make additional notes, and begin writing for the assignment.

Chapter 3

Using the Prewriting Frameworks

This chapter offers general guidelines for planning and using prewriting strategies. I'll begin with teacher-directed activities then move on to student-selected activities. In the next chapter, I'll provide more in-depth sample lesson plans for using the various prewriting frameworks.

When introducing a prewriting framework, provide direct instruction with whole-class participation. You may want to show the prewriting framework on the board, display it on an overhead projector, or distribute photocopies to students. In subsequent lessons using that framework, give students a quick review before getting them started. Eventually, students should be able to use each framework independently and choose an appropriate one for a given assignment. In test situations students should choose and use an appropriate planning sheet or graphic organizer on their own.

Teacher-Directed Activities

As you plan your writing lessons, most likely you consider the different students in your class—their abilities and developmental levels, as well as their learning styles. You also think about the kinds of writing assignments you will use.

In Figure 7 (page 27), the prewriting frameworks are organized into six groups. Each group appeals to a different learning style, requires different thinking skills, and/or may fit a particular kind of writing assignment. The rest of this section gives examples of how you might choose planning sheets or graphic organizers that work well for your class.

Figure 7

Prewriting Planning Sheets and Graphic Organizers

Relatively Unstructured Frameworks	Visual Frameworks	Verbally Structured Frameworks
Write Freely Think Brainstorm Acrostic Web/Cluster	Draw Sketch and Label Imaging	Key Words Key Words Extended Linking Questions Recall Story Map

Frameworks for Grouping Ideas	Oral Frameworks	Frameworks for Analysis
Time Line Outline Categorize Make Notes Paraphrase	Role-Play Interview Questioning	Compare and Contrast Cause and Effect Context Analysis Pros and Cons

27

Considering Students' Abilities and Developmental Levels

You probably find that younger, less-able, or more anxious students need more structure, more direct instruction, and more interactive opportunities than older, confident students. These less-able students might be most successful with the groups of frameworks that invite oral discussion or are verbally structured. Verbally structured organizers, such as **Linking Questions**, are especially useful for these students when the assignment is not based entirely on personal experience.

For instance, fourth graders were asked to write a creative story about a "runaway present." After some discussion with the class and with a partner, Matt began planning his story, using the **Linking Questions** framework *(right)*.

Name ____ Matt ____ Date ____ 2/12/04

Linking Questions

Write the topic below and answer the questions in the boxes. Use the "How" and "Why" boxes to explain your responses in the "What" box. In the "What" box, number the events in order of importance. At the bottom of the page, write a topic sentence based on your responses.

TOPIC: ____ The Runaway Present ____

1. When?
a few days
before Christmas

2. Where?
Snowbern's house in
Merryville, & North Pole

3. Who?
the present = Little Blue, Snowbern family including
Grover the bad kid, Santa, elves, other presents

4. What?

5. How?
Little Blue lands in Santa's
"lost & found" box.

6. Why?
Grover threw
Little Blue away.

_____
_____
_____
_____

Vocabulary
by Matt

bad-tempered   tripped
decorator   rescue
inspector   stacked
rummaging   wobbled
slithered   skittered
bumped   squeaked

After looking over Matt's filled-out organizer, his teacher asked him if there were key words he would like to use. She suggested that Matt write five to ten vocabulary words that would strengthen his descriptions *(left)*.

Then the teacher asked Matt to answer the question "What?" and note at least two events in the story *(right)*.

3. Who?
the present = Little Blue, Snowbern family including
Grover the bad kid, Santa, elves, other presents

4. What?
Snowberns wrap empty boxes. Grover throws
Little Blue away. Santa saves Little Blue.

5. How?
Little Blue lands in Santa's
"lost & found" box.

6. Why?
Grover threw
Little Blue away.

Younger or less-able students are comfortable with visual and oral frameworks. Take a look at this example that uses **Draw** as a prewriting strategy:

For the first writing assignment of the year, a teacher asked her third graders to describe a scene from their lives. "It can be something that happened this summer, or something that happened years ago," she said. "It is like turning photographs into words." The teacher showed a photograph of herself in the woods, with a black bear just behind her. "Does the picture tell a story?" she asked.

Anthony replied, "A bear is chasing you."

"Yes, but to tell the whole story, I'd have to tell you what happened just before and right after the picture was taken," the teacher continued. "This picture is the middle of the story."

She went on to tell the story, with drama and visual imagery. Then she gave students graphic organizers to draw the beginning, middle, and end of their stories. The students put in speech bubbles and wrote summary sentences underneath.

Anthony's scene explained how he fell off his bicycle and had to go to the hospital to get stitches in his knee *(right)*. From this prewriting framework he went on to write a well-organized, interesting account of his personal experience.

Anthony's mother, a second-grade teacher, was surprised by the amount of detail in Anthony's finished story, saying, "He's a very reluctant writer." However, after this first success, Anthony became less and less reluctant as the year continued.

29

While you might use relatively unstructured frameworks with younger or less-able students, use them in conjunction with a more structured framework. For instance, if the assignment requires students to explain photosynthesis, the **Brainstorm** or **Web/Cluster** frameworks might trigger memory of vocabulary or linkages, but **Sketch and Label** might be more effective (see page 54).

Younger students need to be given printed prewriting frameworks and repeated instructional practice before they can use a variety of frameworks independently.

When you teach the higher-order thinking skills in the frameworks used for grouping ideas and analysis, you lead students from simple concrete tasks to more abstract examples. While fifth and sixth graders should have mastered many skills in analysis and synthesis, third graders are still learning, as we can see in the examples below:

After reading a story together, a third-grade class was asked to write a character study. Each student brainstormed about a character he or she had chosen. When finished, the class looked at their lists and decided to categorize their ideas. They agreed to use a color code to identify actions, appearance, motives, important objects, and predictions, circling each item with the appropriate color. The box on page 30 shows how Anthony brainstormed about a character named Ramon. He then used the categories the class agreed on to organize his writing.

Brainstorming about Ramon
by Anthony

R Ramon found a red gull
Y Puerto Rican boy
R Went on a sort of bus
B Liked the beach
Y Black hair, shorts, T-shirt
G Wounded gull
B Liked animals
P Will go home and explain to his mother
P Might go back to the research station
P Might grow up to be a scientist

R He went to the beach
B Wanted to find out about gull
R Went to research station
R Found out about migration
R Met a lot of people on the bus
B Curious, smart, friendly
G Box for gull

Code:
Red = action   Green = object   Yellow = appearance
Blue = motive   Purple = next/prediction

While all students, like Anthony, can use brainstorming successfully, fifth and sixth graders can use more sophisticated prewriting frameworks. In a sixth-grade class, the teacher suggested that students be analytical and persuasive in responding to the following prompt:

Write a speech to give to the PTO, discussing the importance of either music or physical education. Use convincing arguments and anecdotes so that the PTO will work on your behalf to keep the program funded in your school.

Name Maureen   Date 3/16/04

Context Analysis

This planning sheet is useful for elaborating on a science or social studies topic. Write the topic here. Then answer each question below.

TOPIC: Music

1. What are its characteristics? What is it like?
sound singing instruments shows listening reading music
playing instruments fun musicians composers composing

2. How has it changed over time?
Then: mostly just singing to piano, rhythms, listening to records
Now: see #1. Also using computer music programs to compose.

3. How is it a part of something else?
Break in regular classes
Helps with math
Gives people success (might not be good at regular class work)

4. How does it influence other things or people?
Our parents and friends come to concerts and shows.
Some kids grow up to be musicians or singers.
Music helps to settle your feelings if you're having a bad day.

5. Why is it important?
All the notes so far. Music is part of everyone's life.
School teaches us for life. We should have music in school.

Because the sixth graders had used a variety of prewriting frameworks, and were developmentally more capable of analytical thinking, they decided that an appropriate framework would involve **Context Analysis**. Maureen, one of the students, made the prewriting notes at left. You can tell from Maureen's prewriting that she was ready to write her speech.

You know your students well and can help them succeed by choosing the kinds of prewriting frameworks appropriate to their abilities and developmental levels.

Considering Students' Learning Styles

While we all learn from visual, kinesthetic, and auditory stimuli, we each have a preferred learning style. From watching your students, you probably have a good idea of their learning styles. So if someone gets stuck and needs your help, you can guide him or her to use a prewriting framework that matches his or her dominant learning style.

Visual learners enjoy the **Draw, Sketch and Label**, and **Imaging** frameworks. Reluctant writers enjoy these approaches, too, and may be coached into greater productivity if they start with drawing and move up to creating storyboards.

For his science class, Joey had to explain the states of matter. After some coaching from his teacher, Joey remembered "water" and "gas," and drew them, labeling each sketch *(right)*.

His teacher then asked, "What's the third one? Those geometry blocks on my desk aren't water or gas. What are they?"

Joey drew two blocks and wrote, "Solid, like wood."

"Wood is an example of a solid," explained his teacher. "So water is an example of ...?"

"Liquid," said Joey, writing it. Then he inserted "is a" and capitalized "water."

After a bit more coaching Joey was ready to write.

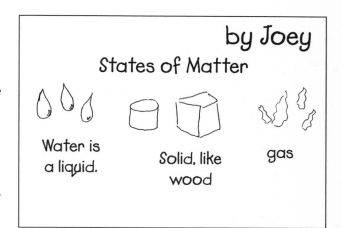

by Joey
States of Matter

Water is a liquid.

Solid, like wood

gas

States of Matter
by Joey

There are 3 states of matter.
One is a liquid like water.
In liquid the little bits roll over
each other.
Two is a solid like wood.
In a solid the little bits
are tight, but shake a
bit sometimes.
Three is a gas like oxygen.
In a gas the little bits are
loose and they bump into
each other.

When Joey wrote his paper *(left)*, he left enough space to draw his pictures "because then the kids will understand," he explained.

By using **Sketch and Label** for science assignments, visual learners have a clearer idea of what needs to be done and can reduce the amount of writing required. **Imaging**, another visual framework, may be developmentally difficult for third graders, but you may find that using symbols rather than pictures helps students move from concrete to abstract thinking. Try imaging a physical activity to give instructions or explain a process, especially to learners who are both visual and kinesthetic.

For instance, in a fifth-grade science class the teacher wanted students to apply the principles of simple machines. She posted the prompt below and invited students to imagine themselves in the situation, and quickly write whatever came to mind using the **Write Freely** framework:

Imagine you are taking a shortcut through the woods when a tree topples, pinning your legs. You are not hurt, but you are stuck. Nearby are other trees, rocks, some fallen branches, and a length of rope. Explain to your science teacher how you can free yourself.

In both examples below you can see that imaging helped students think through some important parts of the situation.

Name _____ Kate _____ Date ___ 4/2/04 ___

Write Freely

Think about your writing assignment for 30 seconds, then begin writing freely about whatever comes to mind—single words, sentences, ideas, your feelings about having to do this. After five minutes, stop. Read what you wrote. Read the assignment again. Highlight valuable ideas or words. Reconsider. List at least three important ideas that will help you organize your writing. Decide on a point of view. Begin writing the assignment.

Stuck so how am I supposed to get free? Help. It's a mess. I don't know. I'll wriggle out. What's the rope supposed to do? Is this a story or science? It's hard. Is the tree heavy? Is that branch strong enough to lever the tree? But what could it rest on?

1._____
2._____
3._____

Name _____ Matt _____ Date ___ 4/2/04 ___

Write Freely

Think about your writing assignment for 30 seconds, then begin writing freely about whatever comes to mind—single words, sentences, ideas, your feelings about having to do this. After five minutes, stop. Read what you wrote. Read the assignment again. Highlight valuable ideas or words. Reconsider. List at least three important ideas that will help you organize your writing. Decide on a point of view. Begin writing the assignment.

Tree – how big? Science teacher – that's a hint. Rope, branches? A pulley? Levers? But if I'm pinned can I reach them? Is it possible? If I sling the rope up over that branch and tie the other end around the tree... No, tie it first. Can I? It's long enough, but I don't know if I can throw it well.

1._____
2._____
3._____

Kinesthetic and auditory learners enjoy the **Role-Play, Questioning,** and **Interview** frameworks, which are particularly useful in social studies. When students ask questions they are more likely to transfer their learning to long-term memory, rather than simply to learn for short-term mastery. For instance, students learning about the American Revolution may have short-term mastery of basic facts by rote memorization, but may acquire a higher level of understanding by questioning. If **Questioning** leads to **Interview** or to **Role-Play,** students may act out events of the revolution and explore the characters of those involved. (The lesson on **Questioning** and **Role-Play** in Chapter 4, page 49, contains an example using the Civil War.)

Students can also have fun making up skits to entertain and teach younger children. In a third-grade class, for example, students were asked to write conflict-resolution plays involving three characters: one character had something and wanted to keep it; a second character also wanted it; and a third character took the side of one of the other characters. In groups of three, using the

Role-Play framework, the students set to work. They chose their own characters, setting, and resolution. The teacher listened in for a few minutes:

Craig:	I'm the Energizer Bunny. I go on and on and on…
Peter:	You're bothering me. I'm Sleepy Squirrel stealing your batteries.
Craig:	Then I'll just stand there and sort of turn a bit and mumble.
Denny:	I'll be the Wise Owl and I'll tell Squirrel to give them back.
Peter:	Only if he stops bothering me.

The boys took on the characters, changing their voices, and getting up to show their movements. They had all their important ideas by the time they began to write.

If you use **Role-Play** to teach script writing, you can revisit those scripts to turn parts of them into a narrative and to practice use of quotation marks and effective use of conversation tags.

Fitting the Framework to the Assignment

Even as you keep in mind students' abilities and learning styles, it is ultimately the writing assignment that most often determines the planning sheet or graphic organizer to be used.

- Stories, poems, and plays may be addressed by structured or unstructured, oral, or visual framework.
- Informational assignments, such as descriptions, instructions, or reports, need frameworks that group or analyze ideas.
- Definitions, explanations, questions, and comparisons may use any organizer, with the choice determined by the content or topic. For instance, questions about seasons might use **Time Line** or **Recall**, but questions about climate might use **Cause and Effect**, **Making Notes**, or **Sketch and Label**.
- A story summary should use a **Story Map**. If students are to summarize a story they have read, they can work in groups, using poster-sized, laminated story-map boards. After the groups have discussed and compared their maps, students can work independently to develop their own maps from which to write their summaries. The laminated boards can be washed off and reused. A biographical summary should also use a **Time Line**.

Student-Selected Activities

Ideally, we would like students to decide for themselves which prewriting framework to use. However before they can do this, they'll need plenty of instruction and practice. Then they can begin to make choices.

Students' learning styles will probably influence their choice, especially the first few times they work on their own. Or they may just use **Brainstorm** because they think that's easy. However, with experience, they realize that if they use **Brainstorm** they may still have to use a second prewriting framework to help them organize their ideas.

Students learn that they have to understand the assignment in order to plan effectively. When students have a written prompt, success depends to a large extent on reading-comprehension skills. When students can paraphrase an assignment you know that they understand it and will think about all the domains as they draft and revise their work, as Mary demonstrates in the next example:

In a fifth-grade class, the teacher reminded her students that when they take a test they would be on their own. She explained, "I will write the prompt on the board and give you the **Paraphrase** framework. You will each work independently to complete the framework. In the prompt you will see in parentheses 'a particular country, city, or area.' You need to choose a real place to substitute for that group of words."

> *A travel agency is looking for exciting vacation destinations. Imagine that the agency asks you about (a particular country, city, or area). Write an account that describes the interesting experiences you had there. Write so that other people would want to go there, too.*

Mary asked, "Should I do Atlantic City or New Jersey?"

The teacher answered, "Think about what the prompt says: a vacation destination. That's all I'm going to tell you for now. I'd like you to try this on your own."

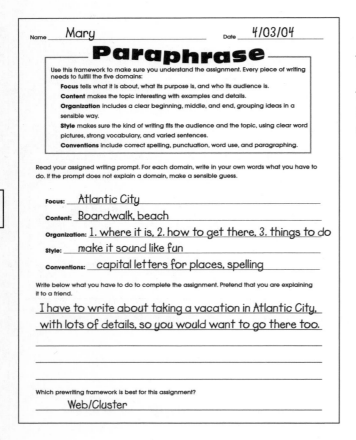

Mary read the directions on the prewriting framework and paraphrased the assignment *(left)*.

Following discussion the students chose a second framework for prewriting. Mary chose **Web/Cluster,** Maureen selected **Imaging,** and David started a memory chain to **Recall** ideas.

Even with practice and encouragement, students may "forget" to use a prewriting planning sheet or graphic organizer. You might remind them how useful they are, as this fifth-grade teacher did when she wrote this assignment on the board and told the class to get busy:

> *Picture yourself awakened as a frog. Write a story to a human friend telling what your new life is like.*

Without using time to plan, students took various approaches *(see next page):*

Kate

Ugh! A frog??!! Wet, slimy, eating flies. Oh yuk.
And I don't even know how to swim.
Who's going to kiss me to bring me back to normal?
What if I get eaten by a snake or a heron?

David

I am a frog. I am part of a food web in a pond. I eat bugs, and could be eaten by a snake or heron.

The teacher stopped the class and asked her students to share with a small group. When they discovered each student's different approach, they wondered whether they could all be right and whether they needed to think again. After some discussion, the students decided that the writing prompt could be addressed in several ways, but they needed to use prewriting frameworks to clarify and organize their ideas. Kate used a **Story Map**, David made notes on a **Time Line**, and Maureen used **Imaging** on a **Web**.

You may begin with a teacher-directed activity that leads to a student-selected activity. In this next example the fifth-grade teacher asked her students to work in small groups to develop materials to teach first graders either about seasons or about climate. She posted the standards criteria on the board *(right)*.

Focus: explain to first graders either seasons or climate

Content: use facts, illustrations, and examples

Organization: sensible sequence

Style: vocabulary suitable to audience

Conventions: spelling, punctuation

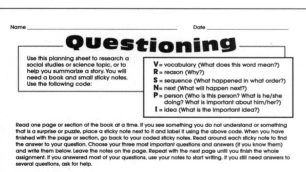

Name _____   Date _____

Questioning

Use this planning sheet to research a social studies or science topic, or to help you summarize a story. You will need a book and small sticky notes. Use the following code:

V = vocabulary (What does this word mean?)
R = reason (Why?)
S = sequence (What happened in what order?)
N = next (What will happen next?)
P = person (Who is this person? What is he/she doing? What is important about him/her?)
I = idea (What is the important idea?)

Read one page or section of the book at a time. If you see something you do not understand or something that is a surprise or puzzle, place a sticky note next to it and label it using the above code. When you have finished with the page or section, go back to your coded sticky notes. Read around each sticky note to find the answer to your question. Choose your three most important questions and answers (if you know them) and write them below. Leave the notes on the page. Repeat with the next page until you finish the whole assignment. If you answered most of your questions, use your notes to start writing. If you still need answers to several questions, ask for help.

Seasons

R: reason – Why does the weather change with the seasons? Why more/less daylight, summer/winter? Earth rotation, tilt on axis, earth around sun, 365 days

S: sequence – spring, summer, fall, winter – 1.What are they like? 2. What makes the changes?

V: vocabulary – axis, rotation, equinox. Too hard for 1st grade. Explain with easy words & pictures

I: important idea – picture books show plants, animals, people for each season

Using a variety of resource materials in the library, including simple picture books, students worked in pairs to use the **Questioning** framework *(left)*, using sticky notes to identify the kinds of questions their materials should answer for first graders. The students then chose their prewriting frameworks and explained their choices.

Jeff liked **Cause and Effect**, planning to make a book with each page having an important idea and a picture or diagram. Colleen and Maureen used **Sketch and Label**, planning to make a poster for each season with diagrams and pictures. David and Jay wanted to **Interview** the first-grade teacher to find out what the class knew already. Then they would **Categorize** things for each season, and create cards that the first graders could sort out, like a game.

When students select or create their own assignments, they have a general idea of what they want to accomplish. If you have posted a list of the prewriting frameworks (as in Figure 7, page 27), and have a file of the photocopied sheets at hand, students will choose planning sheets and graphic organizers that match their learning styles and the type of writing they have in mind.

By the third semester of fourth grade, students will have learned to use most of the planning sheets and graphic organizers. Given the opportunity to work independently in a writers' workshop, some students may look through their journals for ideas. Others may look through a box of idea cards and pictures. A few may choose to work on projects or assignments in social studies or science. No matter what students choose to work on, they know that you expect them to use prewriting frameworks to get started. Let's look at some more examples:

Name ___Kate_____   Date __5/5/04_____

Key Words

Write the topic below. In the first column, list nouns that relate to the topic. List verbs in the second column. Share your list with a partner, then with a small group. Add to your lists. Are there words that show movement, action, or feelings? Are there words that help to explain?

TOPIC: ___Outside the Window_____

Nouns (naming words)	Verbs (action words)
trees	swaying
fence	guarding
vines	twisting

Highlight 5 strong nouns and 5 vivid verbs. Briefly write about the topic below, using at least three nouns and three verbs.

Kate wanted to write a poem about the scene outside the classroom window. At first she tried **Brainstorm**, but had few ideas. She knew that she would be more successful if she had a word bank, so she decided to use the **Key Words** framework, and began by listing nouns and verbs *(left)*.

When Kate extended her lists to include adjectives and adverbs *(next page)*, she felt confident that she had a word bank to help her write her poem.

Kate continued working on her prewriting until she had included the things in the scene that were most important to her. Then she used and rearranged the groups of words she liked the best.

Name __Kate_____ Date __5/6/04__

Key Words Extended

Write the topic below. List adjectives, nouns, verbs, and adverbs that relate to the topic. Share your list with a partner, then with a small group. Add to your lists. Are there words that show movement, action, or feelings? Are there words that help to explain?

TOPIC: ___Outside the Window___

Adjectives	Nouns	Verbs	Adverbs
pink, white, lilac, metal, see-through green	trees fence vines	swaying guarding twisting	gently seriously round the fence

Highlight at least two words in each column. Briefly write about the topic below using some of the words you highlighted.

_____

_____

_____

While Kate was willing to go ahead with her writing, some students were reluctant.

Mike and Jeff were having an argument about Rollerblades and bicycles, not thinking about writing at all, until the teacher intervened.
"You can stay with your discussion, but put it in writing," she suggested.
The boys picked up their pencils, but continued to talk.
Jeff said, "Blades are faster, and you can turn better, too."

"I guess we're comparing," replied Mike. "So we'll use that organizer with the columns."
The boys started their prewriting, noting "Speed?" as their first question, and jotting notes for Rollerblades and bicycles in the appropriate columns.
"What do we write for the both column?" asked Jeff. "They can both go fast."
"It depends how hard you push," answered Mike. "For both of them, I guess."
After a few minutes, the boys had several categories of questions comparing and contrasting Rollerblades with a bicycle *(below)*.

Whether you are giving the class a structured writing assignment or asking students to select a topic for themselves, you know that they need to generate and organize ideas, and they will do so using the prewriting planning sheets and graphic organizers that you have taught.

Name __Mike and Jeff_____ Date __5/17/04__

compare and Contrast 2

Asking key questions is an effective way to find similarities and differences between two things. At the top of columns 2 and 4, write the names of the two items you are comparing. In the first column, write a question on each row. Answer the questions for each item, noting the unique characteristics (differences) in columns 2 and 4. Note the ways in which the two things are similar in column 3.

Questions	Item 1 (differences) Roller Blades	Both items (similarities)	Item 2 (differences) Bicycle
Speed?	really fast	depends how hard you push, & if it's downhill	really fast
Turning?	tight, easy	need to brake & balance	need wider space
Safety?	need pads, not allowed on road	helmet, have to be careful	know road safety rules

37

Sample
Lesson Plans

In this chapter, we'll look at some sample writing lessons that use the various planning sheets and graphic organizers in this book. Lessons are presented in the order in which the frameworks are listed in Figure 7 (page 27). In some cases, more than one framework is used in a lesson.

I suggest grade levels in the lesson plans. However, since ability levels and curriculum content vary from one school district to another, some lessons may be appropriate for a different grade level.

I have also listed standards criteria for the five domains of writing quality: focus, content, organization, style, and conventions. These criteria determine how students will revise their work and how they will be graded. Therefore, I find it helpful to post the criteria for the assignment and/or ask students to note the criteria on their prewriting papers. In a test situation, or with older students, you may give a writing prompt and ask students to determine the standards criteria (using the **Paraphrase** framework). I think teachers should always know the criteria for the assignment, since they determine instructional focus.

Acrostic

> **Grade level:** 4 to 6
> **Type of writing:** descriptive poem
> **Topic:** scenic view
> **Standards criteria**
>   **Focus:** scenic view, structured or unstructured poetry
>   **Content:** detailed word pictures
>   **Organization:** choice of any form of poetry
>   **Style:** strong vocabulary
>   **Conventions:** spelling, capital letter to begin each line

Getting Started

Bring in a variety of scenic pictures to share with students (calendars are a great source). Tell students that they will be writing a poem about a particular place that makes a great photograph —in other words, a scenic view, such as a mountain, ocean, or meadow. If they need help thinking of a place, encourage them to use the pictures you brought in for inspiration. Tell students that they will be using an **Acrostic** framework to help them brainstorm about their topic. (Note: If your class has not studied poetry before, you may want to introduce them to different forms of poetry before starting this activity.)

Modeling

To help model how an acrostic works, ask students to come up with a word other than a scenic view; for example, *flowers*. On the board or overhead projector, set up the acrostic by writing the letters of the word, one on each line, going down the board. If necessary, review alliteration with students. Then challenge them to brainstorm words or phrases associated with flowers that begin with the letters on the board.

Sample Acrostic

F	full of scent, fine colors
L	lovely, lacy, looking pretty
O	orange day lilies, open to bees
W	white mums, wonderful
E	everyone likes them, easy to grow sometimes
R	roses, rabbits can't reach them
S	sunflowers, sow seeds in spring

Using the Acrostic

Distribute copies of the **Acrostic** framework (page 70) to each student. Invite students to choose a place to write about and describe or name it in two or three words (one or two nouns and a verb). When they have their words, encourage them to join with a partner who is working on the same kind of place. Remind students that this process is like brainstorming, so they shouldn't criticize any ideas, including their own.

Name __Ivanna__   Date __10/2/04__

Acrostic

Write the assignment topic as one or two nouns and a verb. List the letters of each word in the boxes below. Use those letters to begin words or phrases that relate to the topic.

TOPIC: __Fog on a mountain, near a city__

F	fog, float, fast cotton balls
O	over mountain, over bridge
G	gray, ghostly, gone if the sun comes out
M	mountain
O	opaque
U	under, over, soft umbrella
N	no noise, makes me nervous
T	thick, thundery, on top, threat
A	awesome, angry, aiming clouds
I	I don't want to live there
N	nearer every minute

Highlight your best ideas. Number them in the order in which you will use them in your writing.

Group Sharing

After partners have worked together for about 10 minutes, divide the class into small groups to share and discuss their work so far. If students don't initiate the use of a thesaurus, suggest that they use one. Allow students to work together until most of them have some ideas for each letter in the acrostic.

Class Discussion

Invite students to share some of their ideas with the class:

Maureen: My place is a garden in autumn. For A, I found *auburn*. That's a red color. And for M, I have *mums like burnished gold*. That's what my mom says our candlesticks are like.

Susan: I have a spring meadow. I wrote *singing bird*s for S, and *poking up flowers* for P.

Colleen: I have a volcano. I got something for all the letters. I wrote: *very hot*; *oh, an explosion*; *lava*; *crimson*; *angry gold*; *nasty ashes*; *oh, so dangerous*.

Teacher: How did the acrostic help you?

Colleen: I could write the important word right away. So it got me started.

Maureen: At first it was hard because my word was *autumn* and I wanted to use colors like red and orange that didn't start with the right letters. That made me use the thesaurus and I ended up with better words.

Looking at the Standards

After students have brainstormed strong vocabulary words, encourage them to turn their notes into a poem. If you haven't done so already, write the standards criteria on the board (page 39) and discuss each criterion with the class.

Teacher: We have colors, actions, and moods or feelings. Now you need to think how to turn these notes into a poem.

Maureen: I want to use the kind of poem we learned that looks like a diamond.

Susan: I don't like any of those kinds of poems—haiku, cinquain, and diamante. I just want to write my own.

Mary: So do I, but how will I know if it's really a poem?

David: You could make it rhyme.

Susan: But you don't have to. You do have to make really good word pictures. You know, with things you can see and feel and hear.

David: No wimpy words.

Maureen: Count the syllables. Make the words make a pattern.

Mary: OK, I think I can try writing now.

Relatively Unstructured Frameworks
Web/Cluster, Time Line

Grade level: 4 to 5
Type of writing: informational, personal experience
Topic: field trip
Standards criteria
    Focus: the field trip (not the bus ride)
    Content: several ideas with interesting information
    Organization: three or four organized paragraphs
    Style: varied sentences, content-specific vocabulary
    Conventions: spelling, punctuation

Getting Started

Before a scheduled field trip, tell the class that they will be writing about the trip. As soon as you return to school, or first thing the next morning, get the class started on prewriting. Tell students that they will be using three different kinds of prewriting frameworks to help them write about the field trip, starting with a **Web/Cluster**. (Note: This lesson assumes that students have not written such a structured field trip report before. Therefore, there is a great deal of teacher direction with students working as a whole class. Students who have used the prewriting frameworks before may need less direction.)

Modeling

On the board or overhead transparency, start the **Web** by writing "field trip" at the center and drawing a circle around it. Explain to students that "field trip" is the main topic. All around the topic, they will be noting things they remember about the trip, including particular places, what they saw, what they did, and what they liked.

Teacher:	Give me some ideas, please.
Jeff:	The State Museum.
Kate:	Dioramas, like Colonial Times and Native Americans.
Laura:	I liked the shop.

As students make suggestions, write their ideas on the board or transparency. Show them how to turn the ideas into a web by drawing lines to join ideas that belong together.

Using Web/Cluster

Distribute copies of the **Web/Cluster** framework (page 94) to students. Encourage them to use the ideas you brainstormed as a class and to add more ideas of their own on the **Web**.

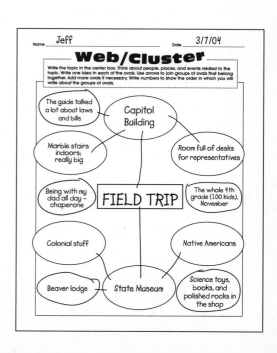

Looking at the Standards

After students have completed their **Webs**, distribute writing paper. Have students copy the standards criteria (page 41) in the top left corner of the page, and their name and date on the top right corner. Discuss the standards with the class.

Teacher:	Let's look at the organization. You need three or four paragraphs. What do you think goes in each one?
Matt:	The first paragraph tells where we went, and when and why.
Laura:	And the last paragraph is your opinion, like your favorite part. So I can tell about the shop.
Jeff:	And the middle ones tell all about what we saw: one for the museum and one for the Capitol Building.
Kate:	That's a lot. I'm just doing three paragraphs. I'll write about the museum but not about that other place.
Teacher:	It's up to you. But remember that you have to meet all the criteria, so you need interesting information and strong vocabulary. Right now, though, you need to get your ideas organized for the paragraphs. In this case, getting organized means putting information in order—according to the time it happened. So we'll use a **Time Line**.

Using Time Line

Photocopy and distribute the **Time Line** framework (page 93) to each student. Have students divide the **Time Line** into four equal sections. Ask them to describe the places that they saw in the order in which they visited them, taking important content from their **Web** and adding details.

Class Discussion

Teacher:	Now we will use linking questions to write the first paragraph. In the first section of your **Time Line**, write where, when, who, and why. Then fill in the answers. Who can use that information to write one single sentence? Try writing it as your first paragraph of your draft. Matt, please read your sentence aloud.
Matt:	"On Wednesday, November 9, 2002, all three 4th grade classes went to Harrisburg to visit the Capitol Building and the State Museum."
Kate:	That can't be the whole first paragraph. It's only one sentence.
Teacher:	If you look in books, you'll see paragraphs of only one sentence. Matt does have a sentence that is fine for his first paragraph. You could add a second sentence if you like. On your **Time Line**, make notes for your final summary/ opinion paragraph, and then go on with your draft.

Verbally Structured Frameworks

Key Words Extended, Story Map

> **Grade level:** 4 to 5
> **Type of writing:** narrative description
> **Topic:** animals in motion
> **Standards criteria**
> **Focus:** two animals in motion (playing tag)
> **Content:** at least five actions
> **Organization:** clear beginning, middle, and end
> **Style:** at least 10 vivid verbs and adverbs
> **Conventions:** simple sentence punctuation, spelling for core words

Getting Started

Prior to this mini-lesson, you may want to read to the class several fiction and nonfiction stories about animals. Focus on the way animals move and elicit students' help in generating a list of adverbs and verbs of motion, such as *gallop*, *trot*, *scurry*, *quickly*, *suddenly*, and *sneakily*. Then tell students that they will be writing a story about animals, using some really strong words to show how animals move. To help them organize their work, they will be using a graphic organizer called **Key Words Extended**.

Modeling

Draw four columns on the board or on a blank transparency with the following headings: adjective, noun, verb, and adverb. Photocopy and distribute copies of **Key Words Extended** (page 81) to each student. Invite students to name an animal and fill in the columns on the board, working together for the first two or three sets of words.

Teacher:	Who will suggest an animal?
Desmond:	A mouse.
Teacher:	How does a mouse move?
Megan:	It scurries.
Teacher:	How does he scurry?
Ariel:	Happily.
Teacher:	How shall we describe this mouse? What kind of mouse is he?
Ariel:	He's a quiet mouse.
Teacher:	So a good sentence might be: "The quiet mouse scurried happily."

Using Key Words Extended

Have students continue filling out their graphic organizers. Make sure each student writes key words for at least three animals. Then ask them to write a sentence about one of the animals, using all the words in that set.

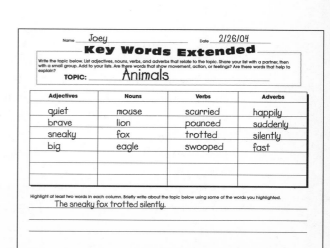

43

Distribute thesauruses to help students come up with more words. Ask them to look up the word *run* and see how many words with similar meaning they can find. You may even want to call on some volunteers to demonstrate four or five of those words, inviting the class to identify each word acted out. Then challenge students to find more verbs that show movement and add them to their lists.

Example of Alphabet Board for Animal Tag Verbs or Motion

A amble	N
B bounce	O
C crawl, creep	P
D dance, dawdle	Q
E edge around	R run
F fall	S scamper, slide, swing
G gallop	T turn, tumble
H hurry	U
I inch along	V
J jump	W wriggle
K	X
L	Y
M move	Z zoom

Group Sharing

Divide the class into small groups. Challenge each group to fill an "alphabet board" of movement words (at least one for each letter of the alphabet) using their own lists and the thesaurus. Encourage students to think of animals from different environments, such as land, air, water, ice, mountains, and underground. Allow 10 minutes for this activity.

Before students go back to their desks, ask them to choose a word from their alphabet board that they could act out and spell for the class. Invite volunteers to mime their words for the class to guess, and then spell the words. Have students add verbs to their prewriting list so that they have at least ten strong action words.

44

Looking at the Standards

Copy the standards (page 43) on the board or a transparency, and review each criterion with the class.

Invite students to select two animals that live in the same environment, such as an ant and a centipede in their backyard. Tell students that they will be using a **Story Map** to plan their characters, setting (time, place), idea or problem of the story (playing tag for fun).

Using Story Map

Photocopy and distribute the **Story Map** graphic organizer (page 91) for each student. Pair up students to write their **Story Maps**. Have students refer to their **Key Words Extended** sheet as they write. After students have filled in the setting, characters, and problem in their **Story Maps**, encourage them to use that information to write the introductory sentence for the story. For the middle of the story, ask them to write five appropriate action verbs. For the end of the story, have them write a concluding sentence, inventing an interruption to the game such as the weather or a new animal suggesting a different game. After students have written their drafts, ask them to highlight their ten vivid words in yellow and their five action words in green. If students are willing, encourage them to role-play with a partner to make sure they have at least five actions words.

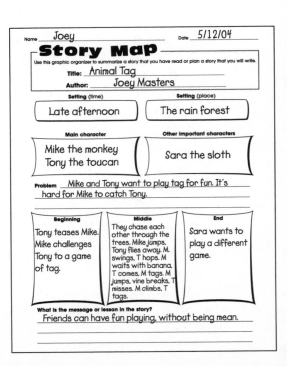

Verbally Structured Frameworks
Recall, Context Analysis

> **Grade level:** 5 or 6
> **Type of writing:** informational
> **Topic:** recycling
> **Standards criteria**
> > **Focus:** accurate information on recycling in the neighborhood
> > **Content:** an understanding of the importance of recycling and the consequences of inaction
> > **Organization:** ideas grouped sensibly, e.g., by type of recycled object
> > **Style:** first like a factual news article, second like a persuasive speech
> > **Conventions:** spelling, paragraphing, punctuation

Getting Started

For this assignment, students write about the same topic twice: first as a news article, then as a persuasive speech. The two styles should be addressed in mini-lessons prior to this assignment. You'll also find it helpful to have previously discussed human interaction with the environment, pollution, and recycling. Write the following prompt on the board:

45

First, explain recycling as it is carried out in this neighborhood, as if writing a short newspaper article. Second, imagine that the township is going to stop recycling because they say it's too expensive. Write a speech to persuade the mayor either to continue recycling or to stop it.

Looking at the Standards

After reading the prompt together as a class, invite students to think about some of the standards criteria they might consider while writing:

Teacher: Let's see if you can suggest some of the standards criteria. On your prewriting paper, list the domains: focus, content, organization, style, and conventions. For organization and style you will probably need two columns. Why?

David: Because we're writing two assignments, and one is like a science explanation, and the other is a speech.

Maureen: And the speech has to be persuasive.

Kate: Focus is first. That's recycling just in this neighborhood.

Colleen: Where do we put the consequences, like what happens if everyone recycles well, or if we end up with big landfills?

Maureen: I think that's content. It's the details and examples.

Teacher: Take a few minutes to fill in the criteria. Then I'll show you what I have.

Write the standards criteria (above) on the board or a transparency. Discuss each criterion with the class, adding appropriate ideas suggested by students, to make sure everyone is in agreement.

Name __Zachary__ Date __5/22/04__

Recall

Use this framework to review what you already know about a topic. After you have jotted down notes in the first five boxes, read the assignment again. Think about the focus, the type of writing, and how you might organize your ideas. Highlight your best ideas and number them in the order you will use for your paragraphs. In the last box, write your introductory sentence.

TOPIC: __Recycling in the Neighborhood__

Personal experience

Neighborhood: glass, aluminum, tin cans, plastic (1, 2), paper. I'm the one who has to put them out on Mondays. It's better than when we mixed everything in the garbage cans. We had 3 trash cans every week.

Things I have read

They use plastic to make fleece sweaters. They can use old paper to make new paper. They're running out of places to put all the other garbage.

TV or Movies

Kids in China (I think) take bits out of old computers to get money.

What other people think

My dad says recycling is a waste of time and we have to pay for the extra garbage trucks and we don't get paid back. My teacher says we have to look after the world's resources.

Ideas or words associated with this

Resources, environment, pollution, reuse, waste, dumps full, landfills, years and years to disintegrate, pay now or pay later, we'll run out of natural resources

Sentence that captures the topic

If we don't recycle we'll have too much trash for the garbage dumps, and we'll run out of natural resources.

Using Recall

Photocopy and distribute the **Recall** graphic organizer (page 88) to each student. Ask students to use the sheet to list all the items that are recycled in the neighborhood. They will need to jot down notes in all the boxes. When students have at least one idea in each of two boxes, encourage them to work with a partner. Explain to students that the section called "Sentence that captures the topic" is like a conclusion: What is the best or worst that could happen about recycling?

Using Context Analysis

At this point, you can have students begin writing their drafts or use the **Linking Questions** framework (page 82) to plan their news article, and **Pros and Cons** (page 86) for the persuasive speech. More sophisticated students may benefit from **Context Analysis** (page 76).

Name __David__ Date __4/15/04__

Context Analysis

This planning sheet is useful for elaborating on a science or social studies topic. Write the topic here. Then answer each question below.

TOPIC: __Recycling in the neighborhood__

1. What are its characteristics? What is it like?
   Stuff like glass, paper, plastic, aluminum, and tin cans that have been used are taken away to factories, broken up, and used again. They're made into new things.

2. How has it changed over time?
   Before, all the trash was thrown away together and put in landfills, or dumped in the ocean. Then they just recycled paper. Then they added other stuff.

3. How is it a part of something else?
   It's part of trash pickup. It's part of stopping pollution and saving land and looking after natural resources. It's part of new inventions and giving people new jobs, like turning plastic into fleece sweaters.

4. How does it influence other things or people?
   See #3. If we DO recycle we don't have such big landfills and our resources last longer. If we DON'T recycle in the end the ocean will be a big dump and the beach will be too messy to swim.

5. Why is it important?
   See #4. And everyone should be responsible for looking after our world.

Verbally Structured Frameworks
Make Notes, Story Map

Grade level: 4 or 5
Type of writing: research information, descriptive narrative
Topic: rain forest
Standards criteria
  Focus: accurately describe three animals in three layers, tell of adventure falling through forest layers
  Content: interesting notes on animals, personal actions and reactions
  Organization: sequence beginning, middle, end
  Style: use two different styles (and formats)—creative narrative and scientific notes
  Conventions: paragraph for time and place; spelling, punctuation

---

Getting Started

This assignment begins in the library but is carried out primarily in the computer room. Students need to know ahead of time how to access the Internet and use a word-processing program at the same time that a Web site is open. You may want to bookmark appropriate sites ahead of time. If you don't have computers, use the library and have students differentiate notes from narrative by using colored pencils.

Read aloud *The Great Kapok Tree* by Lynne Cherry, and discuss the different animals in the story. Tell students that they will be writing about rain forests, specifically those in Central and South America, and the animals that live in each layer. To start off, students will be using the **Make Notes** framework (page 83).

Using Make Notes

Photocopy and distribute the **Make Notes** framework to each student. Have students list each layer of the rain forest: emergent, canopy, understory, shrub layer, herb layer, and forest floor. Tell students that they will be doing research in the library, using reference books and computers. Ask them to note two or three animals for each layer, then highlight a favorite in each group.

Make sure students are specific in their list of animals. In the example at right, Jeff named many animals but needs to specify the type of monkeys and birds.

Name Jeff   **Date** 12/11/04

Make Notes

Write the topic below. Make a few quick notes of facts or subheadings suggested by your notes and the assignment prompt.

TOPIC: Rain Forest

- Emergent layer: harpy eagle, morpho butterfly
- Canopy: toucan, monkeys
- Understory: sloth, monkeys, birds
- Shrub layer: anaconda, cheetah, poison arrow frog
- Herb layer: insects, frogs
- Forest floor: leaf cutter ants, armadillo
-
-
-
-

ORGANIZATION (Look at one or two reference books on the topic. List more categories or subheadings.)

1.
2.
3.
4.
5.
6.
7.
8.

Choose the subheadings that make most sense to you. These will be sections or chapters of your work. Highlight these subheadings. Copy them onto 5 x 8 cards, one subheading to a card. Jot your notes on the cards. Remember: Your notes should be more like lists of words or phrases, not sentences in a paragraph. Use your own words.

---

the example at right, Jeff named many animals but needs to specify the type of monkeys and birds.

Have students do research on the Internet to find at least three facts about each animal, beginning with the one nearest the sky. Encourage students to type their notes using a word-processing program, beginning with the animal's appearance. Have students save their work on the computer.

---

by Jeff
Toucan

Bird: yellow beak like banana, feathers are black, yellow, red
Eats nuts and seeds
Makes loud cracking sound

Looking at the Standards

Tell students that they will use their notes as part of a story. Write the following prompt on the board:

Imagine that you are flying over the rain forest of Central or South America when the plane develops engine trouble, and you have to parachute out. You fall into the rain forest and make your way down through the layers. As you go, you make notes on the animals that you see.

Write the standards (page 47) as well, and explain each criterion to students. Emphasize that they are writing an adventure story with accurate scientific information.

Group Discussion

Teacher: Now that you have your list of animals and some notes, you need to plan your Rain Forest Adventure. Use the **Story Map** framework and review your ideas with a partner to make improvements.

Jeff: Central or South America in January, right?

Teacher: Right. What is the problem of the story?

Kate: Climbing down the tree safely.

Teacher: Yes, making your way down through the layers, paying attention to the animals around you. The beginning is very short. What happens?

Jeff: We bail out of the plane.

Teacher: That's the idea. You don't want to describe the plane journey. I think you understand the middle. How about the end?

Kate: We get rescued.

Teacher: Yes, or you may be on your way out of the forest. Wrap it up, but keep the ending short.

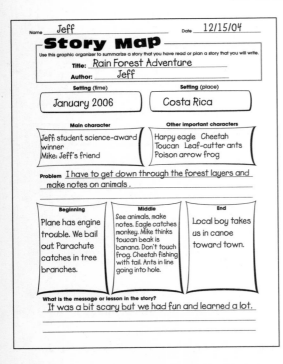

Using Story Map

Photocopy and distribute the **Story Map** framework (page 91) to each student. Ask students to complete their **Story Maps**, and discuss them with a partner. Check students' maps to make sure they are on target.

In the computer room have students retrieve their rain-forest files and write their stories, using a standard font to contrast with their notes, or building their notes into a story. They should improve their notes and drop them into the narrative in the appropriate places. After revising and editing, students may add pictures to the text before printing.

> Excerpt from "Rain Forest Adventure" by Irene
>
> "AUUUUUGGGHH!" Brooke screamed suddenly.
> "What?" asked Martin.
> "THE LEAVES ARE MOVING!"
> Martin looked over at a nearby tree. "Your 'moving leaves' are leaf-cutting ants. They carry leaves back and forth all day. They never stop. They use the leaves for food. They don't eat the leaves. They grow fungus on the leaves and eat it."

Oral Frameworks
Questioning, Role-Play

Grade level: 5 or 6
Type of writing: informative play script
Topic: American Civil War
Standards criteria
    Focus: reasons for fighting the Civil War
    Content: strong characterization; clear, accurate reasons
    Organization: play-script format
    Style: conversational persuasion, no modern slang
    Conventions: format, punctuation, spelling

Getting Started

This activity perfectly complements a study on the American Civil War—an excellent opportunity for students to show what they learned, or a great motivator for disinterested students. Read aloud *Pink and Say* by Patricia Polacco or excerpts from *The Boys' War* by Jim Murphy to the class. Write the prompt below on the board or on a blank transparency:

Write a scene for a play in which the main characters—a Union drummer boy, captured as a prisoner, and a young Confederate guard—explain why they are fighting in the Civil War.

Looking at the Standards

Engage students in a discussion about what they think the standards for this writing assignment should include. Have students write the five domains on a sheet of paper, then give them a few minutes to write their ideas for each domain.

Teacher:	Let's see if we can agree. Who has "focus"?
Mary:	Our job—task—is to write a play. So I wrote, "Play, reasons for Civil War."
Teacher:	That's correct, but I think we need a bit more.
Colleen:	Why are these boys fighting?
Teacher:	Yes, their personal reasons, as well as the big picture—politics. Now, "content"?
David:	Clear reasons, explanations. And I think we should know who the characters are by what they say.
Teacher:	Yes, strong characterization.
Maureen:	Are they arguing? Or is one trying to make the other see his side?
Teacher:	That's up to you. If they volunteered, they may have strong beliefs. In your reading, did you like some boys more than others?
Maureen:	Well, I think the Northerners were right, but I understand where the other side is coming from. The Southerners didn't want the Northerners bossing them around.
Teacher:	So, class, how do Maureen's ideas fit in the standards?
Colleen:	That's part of style and part of content. We don't all have to write about the same kind of people.
Teacher:	Right. The content must include both sides, but how you present them is up to you.

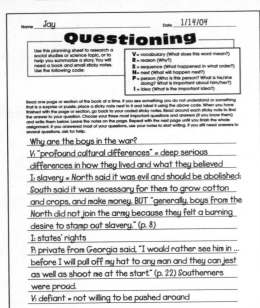

When you and your class have agreed on the standards criteria, write them on the board or transparency so that everyone can refer to them as they write.

Using Questioning

Collect textbooks, copies of *The Boys' War*, and any other relevant materials for students to use as reference. Distribute sticky notes to each student, and copy the **Questioning** code on the board or a transparency. Remind students that with **Questioning**, they're supposed to read only one section at a time. When they see something important or something that they're not sure about, they should put a sticky note next to the passage and code it. When students are finished reading, have them go back and discuss their sticky notes with a partner. Invite students to choose the most important ones and write their notes or questions and answers based on their sticky notes. If students use a quote from the book, remind them to use quotation marks and note the page.

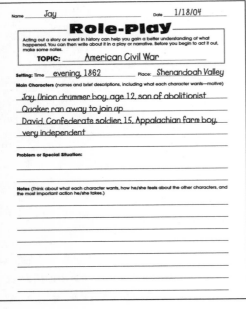

Using Role-Play

Photocopy and distribute the **Role-Play** framework (page 89) to each student. Have students start off by writing their setting —time and place—and the names of their two characters.

Class Discussion

Teacher: Remember that the prompt says that the drummer boy has already been captured. So the play begins when the Confederate soldier comes to guard him. How might the conversation go? Would anyone like to improvise?

(David and Jay volunteer and begin acting out the scene.)

David: "I brought you supper. Not much, half a potato and a bit of rabbit."

Jay: "You don't have good rations either? I thought all the farmers would give you stuff. The fighting's all in your territory."

David: "There are too many of us for the farmers to feed. General Jackson has 17,000 men, and we've been moving through here real fast. We'll beat you Yankees out of our land. You're not going to boss us around."

Teacher: Thank you. Why was that a good beginning?

Maureen: It was realistic. It told us they were in the South.

Colleen: He didn't talk too long about the food. He got into the discussion fast.

Teacher: You may work alone or with a partner. If you're with a partner, you may want to do the same as David and Jay—act a bit, write a bit—to build the scene as you go. If you write alone, get someone to help you act it out when you have a rough draft. Make sure the conversation moves along. Focus on the reasons for the war and the reasons the boys are involved.

Oral Frameworks
Interview

Grade level: 5 or 6
Type of writing: descriptive
Topic: local job/career
Standards criteria:
    Focus: describe a person's job
    Content: details about the job, training, advantages,
          disadvantages, benefits to community
    Organization: sequence topic paragraphs
    Style: job vocabulary, varied sentences
    Conventions: spelling, word choice

Getting Started

Discuss with students about different kinds of jobs and the kinds of businesses that are in your area. Then tell students that they are going to collect some specific information about jobs and write about what they find out. Write the prompt below on the board or a transparency:

Describe the work of a person in your neighborhood and how it benefits the community. Explain the training required, and advantages and disadvantages of this job.

Teacher:	What kinds of jobs might we include? Think about jobs that your parents or neighbors have. Do you think you know enough about one of those jobs to write this assignment? How might you find out the information needed?
Mary:	My mom is a school bus driver, and I know a lot about that.
Teacher:	Could you explain the advantages and disadvantages?
Mary:	Some of them. She doesn't like the kids yelling. But I guess I could ask her some more.
Teacher:	Exactly. You are going to develop an **Interview** framework, conduct the interview, and then write the assignment.

Looking at the Standards

Write the standards criteria (above) on the board or a transparency, and discuss each criterion with students.

Teacher:	The focus is someone's job, but what else do you need? Since the prompt does not name an audience, you need to decide on one. If you tilt the focus toward community benefit because you're describing a local service job, like Mary's mom being a bus driver, you might think of yourself as local newspaper reporter. If you focus on the second part of the prompt you might write like a career counselor.

Modeling

Before distributing the **Interview** planning sheet, you may want to discuss with students about what kinds of questions to ask and how.

Teacher:	You could all use the linking questions: Who? What? Where? When? How? Why? While I was planning this lesson, I asked Colleen if she would help me. She's a baby-sitter, and I'm going to interview her about that job. Before I wrote my questions, I thought about what I already knew. I made some notes. In the interview I would check with her to make sure that my notes were right, but the important questions have to be things I really didn't know. So I started by writing headings: "Training," "Advantages," and "Disadvantages," leaving big spaces between each one for particular questions. Then I thought of some more questions at the end. I'm going to tape-record my interview because, while I can write pretty fast, I may not get everything Colleen says. Ready, Colleen? Did you have special training to be a baby-sitter?
Colleen:	Yes.
Teacher:	Hmm...that wasn't a good question, because I didn't find out much. No more yes/no questions. Colleen, please tell me about the training you had.
Colleen:	I went to Chester County Hospital for a whole Saturday and had training from a children's nurse. I had to take my lunch and a doll as a pretend baby. There were six of us in the class, and we sat around a table and talked.

Continue the interview, making side comments to the class to show that open-ended questions are more successful than those that would elicit single-word answers. Ask questions that find out: How much? Why? How difficult/easy? Encourage students to make suggestions, then write some other general question ideas on the board:

What kind of training did you have?

What are the advantages of this job? To you? To the family? To the community?

Why would someone dislike this job?

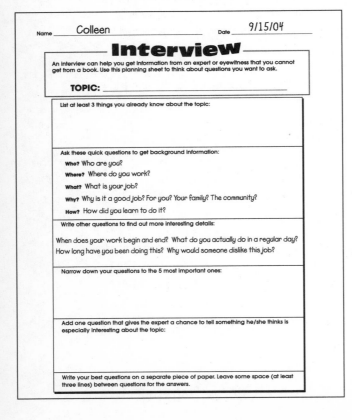

Using Interview

Photocopy and distribute the **Interview** planning sheet (page 79) to each student. Have students decide on a job and the person they will interview. Encourage them to first make notes on what they already know, organizing their notes under topic headings suggested by the content criteria. If students are considering similar jobs, you may want to let them work together on the questions, even though they will conduct separate interviews. If students are working individually, have them ask a friend to read and comment on the questions they have written. Remind students that they need at least five strong questions.

Class Discussion

Divide the class into small groups and encourage students to share their questions with their group. After a few minutes, ask a volunteer from each group to share some ideas with the class.

David: In our group most of our questions were pretty much the same. But then we decided we really had to understand our questions, and we weren't sure how we could ask about helping the community. If the person is a doctor, that's easy, but how do we explain the question to a secretary?

Teacher: It would really be up to the person to answer. But when we think of community help, what could that be? How does a business company help?

Mary: Sometimes they give things to schools.

Maureen: They give people jobs. And the secretary spends her paycheck in our shops.

Teacher: Good ideas. Next group. Colleen.

Colleen: We helped each other fix some questions, mostly by adding hints. Michelle put in a question about what the next step in the job would be. If it went places it would be an advantage, but if it was a dead end it was a disadvantage.

Teacher: Good. Jay, you're next.

Jay: We talked about using the answers. I decided I wanted to write like a guidance counselor, so I needed more questions about training and advantages. Susan says she's going to write something like a congratulations piece, thanking the person for being a firefighter. So she added more questions about community help.

Teacher: Good. Yes, you do need to think ahead as to the focus of your writing—your audience and purpose. Your questions should match your focus. Your homework for the next three days is to complete your interviews and begin the draft.

53

Visual Frameworks
Sketch and Label

Grade level: 4 or 5
Type of writing: summary explanation
Topic: photosynthesis
Standards criteria
    Focus: explain photosynthesis
    Content: briefly, clearly
    Organization: numbered sentences, referring to the diagram
    Style: content-specific vocabulary
    Conventions: spelling

Getting Started

Use this writing assignment to help students review for a test on a topic such as photosynthesis. Tell students that they will be using **Sketch and Label** to explain photosynthesis.

Looking at the Standards

Write the standards criteria on the board and have students copy them on their assignment paper. Explain that they will be drawing a rough sketch for prewriting, and a clearer illustration for the final copy. Discourage students from using a book for reference. At this point, students should know enough about photosynthesis to write about it.

Using Sketch and Label

Photocopy and distribute **Sketch and Label** (page 90) to each student. Have students sketch a diagram explaining photosynthesis. Then have them label each part of their sketch.

Teacher:	Notice that the standards criteria ask you to explain using numbered sentences, referring to the diagram. What does this suggest that you do?
Matt:	Number the labels in the order you want to write about them.
Teacher:	Right. What would be first, and why?
Jeff:	The roots, because they suck up water.
Teacher:	If you begin with the roots, what would be second?
Jeff:	The stem, because it takes water to the leaves, and that's where photosynthesis happens.
Teacher:	If the focus is photosynthesis, do you need to explain the function of the roots? Does anyone have a different idea?
Laura:	I'm beginning with the leaf...well, the water in the leaf. My second is carbon dioxide from the air. I didn't label the roots and the stem because they're not really part of photosynthesis.
Teacher:	You don't all have to have the same thing. But remember that this is a short explanation. Finish the sketch, number and label the parts. Add a few words that explain the function of each part. Stay focused.

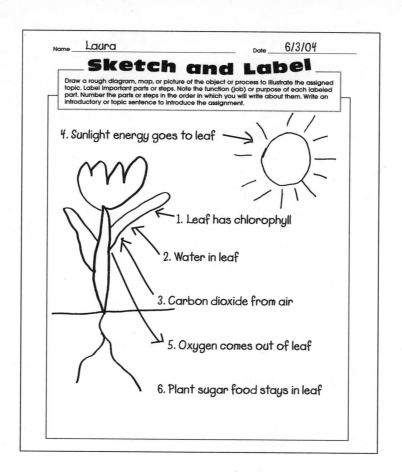

Name ___Laura_____ Date ___6/3/04_____

Sketch and Label

Draw a rough diagram, map, or picture of the object or process to illustrate the assigned topic. Label important parts or steps. Note the function (job) or purpose of each labeled part. Number the parts or steps in the order in which you will write about them. Write an introductory or topic sentence to introduce the assignment.

4. Sunlight energy goes to leaf

1. Leaf has chlorophyll

2. Water in leaf

3. Carbon dioxide from air

5. Oxygen comes out of leaf

6. Plant sugar food stays in leaf

55

Group Sharing

Divide the class into small groups and invite students to share their sketches and ideas with their group. Encourage students to help one another clarify ideas, if necessary.

Teacher: When you share your sketches in your group, don't try to persuade the others to use your sequence. If the owner can explain clearly, that's the important thing. Remember to stick to the point. You are only explaining photosynthesis.

Jeff: I decided to skip the roots and stem. When I write about the water in the leaf, I'll just say, "carried from the roots by the stem."

Teacher: Now go on to your assignment paper. Redraw the sketch tidily, label neatly, and begin to write in numbered order.

Note: The **Sketch and Label** framework is useful not only in science, but also for map skills and for explaining interactive events.

Visual Frameworks

Imaging

Grade level: 3 to 6
Type of writing: descriptive
Topic: favorite activity
Standards criteria
    Focus: description of a favorite activity
    Content: details of action, mood, emotions, location
    Organization: student's choice
    Style: vivid imagery
    Conventions: spelling

Getting Started

Tell students that they will be writing about their favorite activity. They can write a poem, song, rap, story, magazine article—any kind of writing that they like. The important thing is that their description be full of enthusiasm.

Modeling

Copy the **Imaging** framework (page 78) on a blank transparency. Tell students about a favorite activity. As you narrate, use colored markers to fill in the framework.

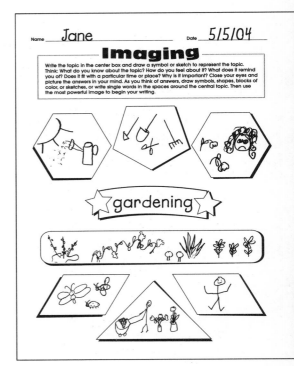

Teacher: My topic is gardening. You can see that I love flowers. My summer garden is full of warm colors of pinks, purples, and soft reds. Bees bumble and murmur lazily. My fall garden is orange, yellow, and red. The bright colors shout at the windswept leaves. I am working, digging, planting, weeding—all sweaty and dirty, but happy. The brown shadow, with my sad face beside it, shows a drought when plants die. The triangle shows me going to buy gardening tools and seeds for next year. This prewriting has symbols and pictures, but no words. Now you try.

Class Discussion

Photocopy and distribute the **Imaging** graphic organizer to each student. Provide colored markers or crayons. Invite students to close their eyes and "see" their hobby or activity, then draw symbols to represent the activity on the graphic organizer. When they're finished, encourage students to write a few words to go with the symbols they drew.

Teacher:	You have some great symbols and pictures here. Now I would like you to write a few words. In our reading we have found similes and metaphors, and we have liked the way word pictures help us appreciate the story. In my example I showed brown as sadness. How could I write that?
Jeff:	You were as sad as a dying plant.
Laura:	Your frown curled up like the dry flowers.
Teacher:	Take a look at your own imaging. Can you find a simile or metaphor?
Matt:	I did playing my violin. One of my pictures is made of music notes turning into birds. I could write, "The music from my violin flies like birds all around my room."
Teacher:	Good. Another example?
Laura:	I did cheerleading. One picture is loads of pom-poms. In a poem, I'll say, "feathery flutters rise and fall like fountains."
Teacher:	Great! Now explain your graphics to a partner, writing phrases as you talk.

Looking at the Standards

If necessary, review the standards criteria with students. Remind students that this assignment calls for a short piece of writing that should be as powerful as their graphic organizers.

by Laura

Cheerleading
Feathery flutters rise
and fall like fountains
Girls climb and
balance to make
mountains

by Kate

Soccer
I run like the wind. I
kick like a kangaroo.
When I score I
dance like a monkey.

57

Frameworks for Grouping Ideas

Time Line, Make Notes

Grade level: 4 or 5
Type of writing: informative
Topic: biography
Standards criteria
    Focus: biography of a famous explorer
    Content: background information, adventures, difficulties,
        conclusion
    Organization: chronological order
    Style: varied sentences, content-specific vocabulary
    Conventions: paragraph for time and place; spelling, capitalization

Getting Started

Follow up a unit on explorers with this writing assignment. Invite each student to choose an explorer to report on. Tell students that they will read more about the explorer they chose and conduct in-depth research to write about his life. Allot about three weeks for students to complete this assignment. Encourage them to work in the library and on computers to gather their research notes into a folder.

Looking at the Standards

Copy the standards criteria on the board or a transparency, and discuss each criterion with the class. Have students copy the standards, keeping the copy in their folder so they can refer to it as necessary. Involve students in a backward mapping activity, using a calendar to determine due dates for their work, including conferencing with you about their notes after about a week. On the board, write the prompt below for students to copy. Make sure students share the prompt as well as the calendar with their parents.

Write a biography of a famous explorer. Include background information, the most important adventures, difficulties and how the explorer overcame them, your conclusion about the importance of the exploration, a time line showing the sequence of important events, and a map showing the places explored.

Group Sharing

If some students are having a difficult time deciding which explorer to focus on, put them in small groups and invite them to take turns telling each other whom they might study and why. After everyone has made a decision, group students according to the explorer they've chosen. Some groups may consist of only a pair of students, while others may include more. Tell students that they will remain in these working groups as they work on their **Time Lines** and **Make Notes**.

Using Time Line

Photocopy and distribute the **Time Line** graphic organizer (page 93) to each student. At the bottom of the **Time Line**, have students write the word "born." At the top, have them write, "died." Have students make small crossing lines every half-inch beginning from the bottom.

Explain to students that when they know the birth and death dates of their explorer, they will be able to decide on the scale value for their **Time Line**. For example, if the explorer lived about 50 years, each inch may be worth five years. If your explorer lived more than 50 years, each half-inch may be worth five years. Encourage students to jot down notes on the **Time Line**. For instance, on the birth date, say where the explorer was born. On the death date, say where and how he died. Remind them to write just the basic facts of the most important adventures or difficulties.

Using Make Notes

When students have completed their **Time Lines**, photocopy and distribute the **Make Notes** planning sheet (page 83). As students begin to write their notes, remind them that some reference books may be organized differently from the way they plan to organize their own report. Have students use their **Time Line** to help them to write their introduction.

Class Discussion

As students continue to do research, check up on them and encourage them to discuss with you any problems or questions they may have.

Teacher: Continue to make notes about your explorer's difficulties and adventures. Use your own words. When you have finished, read through the page and number your notes in the order in which you will write them.

Kate: How do we know when we have enough notes?

Teacher: When you have used at least two kinds of references, such as a Web site, an encyclopedia, or another book, and you are not reading anything new.

Matt: Do we have to tell the whole life story or should we stick to the exploring part? My explorer was in a war before he started exploring. Should I write about the war?

Teacher: No. Stay focused on the exploring. Write the conclusion and your opinion after you have finished the adventures and difficulties.

Before students begin their rough draft, make sure they review their notes with you. Have them write their drafts and final copies on a computer, reviewing with a peer editor and with you along the way.

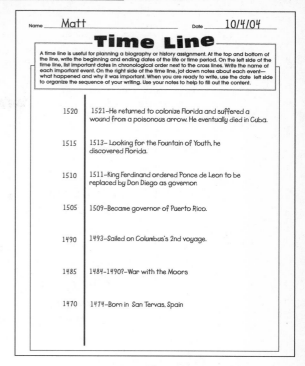

Name _Matt_   Date __10/4/04__

Time Line

A time line is useful for planning a biography or history assignment. At the top and bottom of the line, write the beginning and ending dates of the life or time period. On the left side of the time line, list important dates in chronological order next to the cross lines. Write the name of each important event. On the right side of the time line, jot down notes about each event—what happened and why it was important. When you are ready to write, use the date left side to organize the sequence of your writing. Use your notes to help you fill out the content.

1520	1521–He returned to colonize Florida and suffered a wound from a poisonous arrow. He eventually died in Cuba.
1515	1513– Looking for the Fountain of Youth, he discovered Florida.
1510	1511–King Ferdinand ordered Ponce de Leon to be replaced by Don Diego as governor.
1505	1509–Became governor of Puerto Rico.
1490	1493–Sailed on Columbus's 2nd voyage.
1485	1484–1490?–War with the Moors
1470	1474–Born in San Tervas, Spain

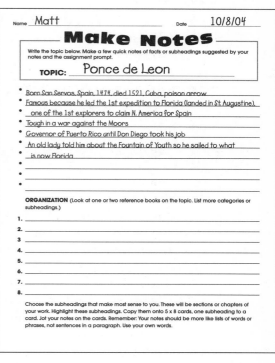

Name _Matt_   Date __10/8/04__

Make Notes

Write the topic below. Make a few quick notes of facts or subheadings suggested by your notes and the assignment prompt.

TOPIC: _Ponce de Leon_

- Born San Servos, Spain, 1474, died 1521, Cuba, poison arrow
- Famous because he led the 1st expedition to Florida (landed in St. Augustine),
- one of the 1st explorers to claim N. America for Spain
- Tough in a war against the Moors
- Governor of Puerto Rico until Don Diego took his job
- An old lady told him about the Fountain of Youth so he sailed to what
- is now Florida
-
-
-

ORGANIZATION (Look at one or two reference books on the topic. List more categories or subheadings.)

1. _____
2. _____
3. _____
4. _____
5. _____
6. _____
7. _____
8. _____

Choose the subheadings that make most sense to you. These will be sections or chapters of your work. Highlight these subheadings. Copy them onto 5 x 8 cards, one subheading to a card. Jot your notes on the cards. Remember: Your notes should be more like lists of words or phrases, not sentences in a paragraph. Use your own words.

59

Frameworks for Grouping Ideas

Categorize

> **Grade level:** 4 or 5
> **Type of writing:** information
> **Topic:** animals
> **Standards criteria**
> > **Focus:** describe one animal, like a third-grade reference book
> > **Content:** detailed, interesting information
> > **Organization:** side heading for each of four to six categories
> > **Style:** varied sentences, strong vocabulary
> > **Conventions:** punctuation, spelling

Getting Started

Tell students that they will be writing a report on an animal over several weeks, using the library for research, reading during silent reading time and for homework, and writing in class. Provide students with 5 x 8 cards for their notes and folders for their materials.

Looking at the Standards

Copy the project guidelines below for students. To ensure that everyone understands what to do, have students take home a copy of the guidelines and explain them to their parents.

Animal Project Guidelines

1. Choose an animal.
2. Learn about it.
3. Choose categories to be used as chapter headings, and set up a note card for each chapter.
4. Make notes on the cards. Ask your teacher to check your notes by _____.
5. Use the notes to write a report, organized under the chapter headings.
6. Succeed on these criteria:
   Focus: describe one animal, like a third-grade reference book
   Content: detailed, interesting information
   Organization: side heading for each of four to six categories
   Style: varied sentences, strong vocabulary
   Conventions: punctuation, spelling
7. Edit and improve your rough draft and ask your teacher to check it.
8. Write the final copy. (You may have help to do it on the computer, but your typist cannot change your work.)
9. Make a colorful cover. Include pictures.
10. Be prepared to share your report with other third graders.
11. Hand in everything by _____.

Encourage students to ask questions if they have any, then help them get organized. Together with the class, use a calendar to create a working time line with a final due date and interim dates for completion and checking sections of the report. At the library, encourage students to ask the librarian for help locating books and other relevant reference materials. Have each student choose a book to use.

Using Categorize

Photocopy and distribute the **Categorize** framework (page 72) to each student. Tell students that they will be using this graphic organizer to help them with their prewriting. Guide them to use the library book they borrowed to help them decide how to organize their report.

Teacher: Look through your library book. Open to the table of contents and the index, and see how the information is organized. Try to find section titles that you might want to cover in your report. Who can make a suggestion?

Megan: What dolphins eat.

Teacher: That's important, but of course each person will study a different animal. How can we take Megan's idea and make it a heading for all animals?

Anthony: What this animal eats. But that's not enough, because in my book it tells how the lion goes hunting, and how it's camouflaged.

Megan: We could say, "What the animal eats, and how it gets its food."

Teacher: So the category is food. Do we all like Megan's question as a heading? On your graphic organizer, write that heading in one of the boxes. When you are reading to find information for that chapter of your report, you will need to find what the animal eats, how it gets the food, where, and when. For instance, a brown bear in Alaska catches salmon with its paw from a river, turns over rocks to find small creatures, and eats a lot in the fall before it hibernates. In the box about eating, write "What? How? Where? When?" Now you have good guiding questions for that category.

Have students work in small groups to decide on three or four more categories of information. Tell students that when they select a category they should see if there are parts to that category, such as the questions you had for food. Remind students to make their category titles general enough for everyone. While everyone may not have identical headings and questions, students should cover the following: appearance, habitat, food, family, and adaptations. For more-advanced students, you may want to suggest a category on interactions with other animals sharing the environment. Assist students with their work as needed.

Encourage students to discuss their ideas with the class. Once students have decided on which animal to report on, they will be making notes on cards. Distribute 5 x 8 cards to students. Tell students to write a category or chapter heading and their cue questions on each card, using the ideas they generated on their graphic organizers. Or, you can elicit suggestions from the class on what headings to use. Once students have made their decisions, group them so that people studying similar animals can share materials.

61

Name Megan   Date 12/2/04

Categorize

Write the main topic in the top box. Think: What are some important parts or sections of the topic? Write each part in each box. For each part, write one or two questions to answer while writing.

Animal report

What the animal eats and how it gets its food. What? How? Where? When?

What does it look like? How big? Color? Are babies different?

Where the animal lives. Kind of place. Kind of home. Does it stay or migrate?

Family. How many babies? What are they like? How do parents look after them?

What special adaptations does it have?

Write a sentence below to show how all the parts belong together.

---

by Megan
What the dolphin looks like:
Size?
Weight?
Color?
Skin covering?
Special shape?
How do the young change as they get older?

Analytical Frameworks
Compare and Contrast

> **Grade level:** 4 or 5
> **Type of writing:** informative
> **Topic:** modern and colonial times
> **Standards criteria**
> > **Focus:** compare and contrast life today with life in colonial times
> > **Content:** include information on at least five categories
> > **Organization:** by topics, plus an introduction and conclusion
> > **Style:** content-specific vocabulary
> > **Conventions:** paragraphing, punctuation, spelling

Getting Started

Use this writing activity in conjunction with a unit on colonial times. Write the following prompt on the board:

Compare and contrast life today with life in colonial times. Consider at least five categories, such as food, water, shelter, communication, education, farming or other occupations.

Looking at the Standards

Copy the standards criteria (above) on the board or a transparency. Give students a few minutes to analyze the writing prompt and study the standards criteria, allowing partner discussion. Invite students to share their discussions with the class.

Kate:	I want to write mine like a table in a textbook, but Laura says that's boring.
Laura:	I want to write a story where one of the characters travels through time.
Teacher:	Could you both be right?
Matt:	I think they could both be right, as long as they compare and contrast. I want to do mine like a debate.
Teacher:	Yes, as long as you compare and contrast, you could organize your work in several different ways. So what exactly does that mean?
Kate:	You tell how the things are different.
Laura:	And you tell how they are the same. Like in third grade when we did Venn diagrams for moths and butterflies.

Modeling

Tell students that in this activity, they are going to look for things that are the same and things that are different. But instead of using the familiar Venn diagram, they will be using a **Compare and Contrast** framework, which will allow them to include more information than they could fit into the circles of a Venn diagram.

Photocopy and distribute **Compare and Contrast 2** (page 75) to each student. Display a transparency copy on the overhead. Point out that the first column is for the questions or categories to be considered. The second column is for colonial times, and the last is for modern times. The column in between is where students should list similarities between the two times.

Together with the class, decide on five questions or categories for the organizer. Lead the class in completing the first question.

Name __Terry_____   Date __10/19/04_____

compare and Contrast 2

Asking key questions is an effective way to find similarities and differences between two things. At the top of columns 2 and 4, write the names of the two items you are comparing. In the first column, write a question on each row. Answer the questions for each item, noting the unique characteristics (differences) in columns 2 and 4. Note the ways in which the two things are similar in column 3.

Questions	Item 1 (differences) Colonial Times	Both items (similarities)	Item 2 (differences) Modern times
Communication?	Type-set printing, broadsides, in cities, not often, town criers;	Newspapers	Computer print, everywhere, daily, TV, radio;
	quills, ink, letters' horseback, not organized;	Mail	ink in pens, letters, US postal system;
	in person, slow, mostly English	Voice	phone, fast, English and many other languages

Using Compare and Contrast

Encourage students to complete the rest of the **Compare and Contrast** graphic organizer.

Teacher: Now that you have an idea of how to compare and contrast, you should add four more questions. The prompt suggests food, water, shelter, education, or an occupation, but you may choose your own if you like.

Kate: Can I do fashion?

Teacher: You could, or you could do clothing, which would include the fabrics as well as the styles. Any other ideas?

David: I thought of travel, but I'd have too much for modern times. I might do transportation by road.

Laura: I think I'll do kitchen equipment, but just for cooking.

Kate: If colonials have a fireplace, and we have a stove, what do they both have?

Laura: Heat energy. They both had ovens, too. Remember the colonial brick oven at the side of the fireplace? Like a pizza oven? And poorer people used a Dutch oven—like a big heavy saucepan with a tight lid.

Kate: Right. But if they both had heat, don't we have to write that colonials burned wood but we use electricity or gas?

Teacher: It sounds as if you have some good ideas. Work with a partner or in a small group if you have similar categories. Use reference materials if you need them.

Class Discussion

When students have finished filling in their graphic organizer, bring the class together again to discuss some formats that they may use to write their drafts.

Teacher:	I know that you are using various formats, but you will need to address one category or question at a time. How will you organize the ideas?
Laura:	I would name the question, like cooking, at the beginning of the section. Then I would look in the "both" column for a subcategory.
Kate:	That sounds like a report. I thought you were writing a story.
Laura:	I am, but I'll still organize my thinking. I could say, "One minute I was standing with a Pyrex dish, ready to put it in the microwave. The next minute I felt a wave of heat near the floor and found myself standing in front of a huge fireplace. I had a wooden spoon in my hand and was stirring a cauldron of stew." So I would be comparing the two kinds of cooking places. My character will do something to show the differences. Then the character will think about it, and I'll show the similarities.
Kate:	You'll have to do more work than I do. I said I'd do a table, and I've done it.
Teacher:	You have a prewriting table of notes. If you choose to use that as part of your completed work, imagine it in a textbook. There would also be some paragraphs discussing the notes in more detail, perhaps explaining why colonials wore only linen or wool, while we have many kinds of fabrics. If you don't want to write discussion paragraphs, you will need to make more detailed tables. Before you begin your drafts, does anyone have anything to say about this prewriting graphic organizer?
Jeff:	I liked it because it is easier to read back than a Venn diagram. There's more space to write.
Matt:	It's more step-by-step than a Venn, but you can sort out ideas really well. It makes you think.

Analytical Frameworks
Cause and Effect

Grade level: 4 or 5
Type of writing: informative
Topic: water cycle
Standards criteria
   Focus: explain the water cycle as a cause-and-effect sequence
   Content: accurate and complete information
   Organization: logical sequence
   Style: content-specific vocabulary
   Conventions: spelling, no fragments or run-on sentences

Getting Started

After a unit on weather and the water cycle, assign students this writing activity to assess their understanding. Tell students that they will be using a **Cause and Effect** graphic organizer to explain the water cycle. Write the following prompt on the board:

Explain the water cycle accurately and completely, using content-specific vocabulary, and following a logical sequence. Use complete sentences.

Looking at the Standards

List the five writing domains on the board, then challenge students to read the prompt carefully and think about what the standards criteria might be. Discuss students' ideas and write them on the board as they match the criteria above. Tell students that they will be using a **Cause and Effect** graphic organizer to help them plan their writing.

Modeling

Photocopy and distribute the **Cause and Effect** graphic organizer (page 73) to each student. Display a transparency copy of the organizer on the overhead or create one on the board. Ask students: *What is the main effect of the water cycle?* When students answer, *"Rain,"* write it in the oval at the top of the transparency sheet and have students do the same in their organizers. As you continue the discussion with students, encourage them to begin jotting down notes in the other spaces on the organizer.

Teacher: Think about what happens immediately before that effect—the rain. What is the first or primary cause? Remember that that cause is itself an effect of something

65

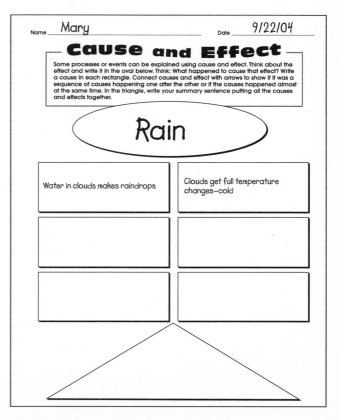

Name __Mary__   Date __9/22/04__

Cause and Effect

Some processes or events can be explained using cause and effect. Think about the effect and write it in the oval below. Think: What happened to cause that effect? Write a cause in each rectangle. Connect causes and effect with arrows to show if it was a sequence of causes happening one after the other or if the causes happened almost at the same time. In the triangle, write your summary sentence putting all the causes and effects together.

Rain

Water in clouds makes raindrops

Clouds get full temperature changes—cold

that happened right beforehand. And so on. We are going to end up with a series of causes and effects. Let's see what we have so far. What makes it rain?

David: The water in the clouds condenses.

Mary: That means the water makes raindrops.

Teacher: Both of you are right, but the assignment prompt asks you to use content-specific vocabulary, so you do need to use the word "condense" or "condensation." Mary's answer puts it in simpler words, which is also helpful to show understanding. So if condensation is also an effect, what caused it?

Mary: The clouds get full. No, that doesn't sound right. I'm thinking of the diagram when the clouds go up as they reach the mountain, and then it rains.

David: The temperature changes.

Teacher: Continue working backwards from the rain until you have completed the cycle. Then connect the boxes with arrows to show the sequence. Write a brief summary sentence in the triangle.

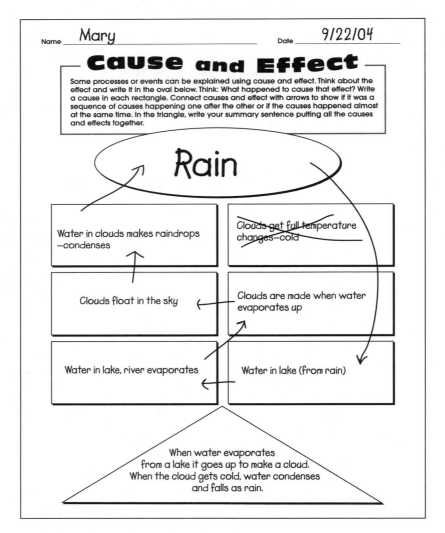

Encourage students to share their completed graphic organizer with a partner. Then have students work on their own to write the assignment.

Analytical Frameworks

Pros and Cons

> **Grade level:** 4 or 5
> **Type of writing:** informative
> **Topic:** technological change
> **Standards criteria**
> > **Focus:** identify and discuss technological change in the community
> > **Content:** give three examples with both positive and negative effects
> > **Organization:** introduction, conclusion, three main paragraphs
> > **Style:** content-specific vocabulary
> > **Conventions:** spelling, paragraphs, no run-ons or fragments

Getting Started

Invite students to close their eyes and imagine themselves in their own bedroom. Ask: *What objects do you see that use energy and that your parents would not have had when they were your age? (Computers, TV, cell phone, and so on)* Tell students that they will be writing about technology and its impact on society.

Looking at the Standards

Write the standards criteria (above) on the board or a transparency, and discuss any questions students may have.

67

Modeling

Teacher: Just before when I asked you to close your eyes, you were imaging. That's like imagining yourself in another place or doing something else. You make pictures in your mind. If I had this assignment when I was your age ... Let me think. I'll close my eyes and be eleven years old ... We just got a black-and-white TV, and it only has programs in the evening. We watch that instead of reading or playing cards with my dad.

Notice that when I made my notes, I listed them under "pro" and "con" for advantages and disadvantages. Another way to think about it is that "pro" means the good things about having this new technology, instead of whatever there was before. The "con" means the bad things about the new technology. When we got the TV, I liked watching some of the programs, but I missed playing family games.

New TV in Living Room	
Pro	Con
Fun, new	Less reading, card games
Up-to-date news	Brothers argue about programs

Using Pros and Cons

Challenge students to think of three kinds of technology that they use in school or at home that their parents did not have. Remind them that they will be writing about changes in the community, and that community is where they live.

Photocopy and distribute the **Pros and Cons** graphic organizer (page 86) to each student. Point out the three sets of rectangles labeled Choice 1, 2, and 3. Have students write one type of technological change for each choice. Next, invite them to think about at least one good thing about each of their choices and write those advantages under "pro."

Teacher:	Who will give me an example?
Jay:	School computers. They're good because we can play cool math games.
Teacher:	Now imagine an adult who thinks that you should not have computers in school. How would he argue with you? What disadvantage would he suggest?
Jay:	He'd say we shouldn't play computer math games, that we should do problems out of the book.
Teacher:	So what is the disadvantage? How would you write it?
Jay:	Games aren't serious learning. I'd write it, but I don't believe it.
Teacher:	That's OK. You are showing you see the other point of view. With a partner, or in groups of three, find at least two advantages and two disadvantages for each of your three choices.

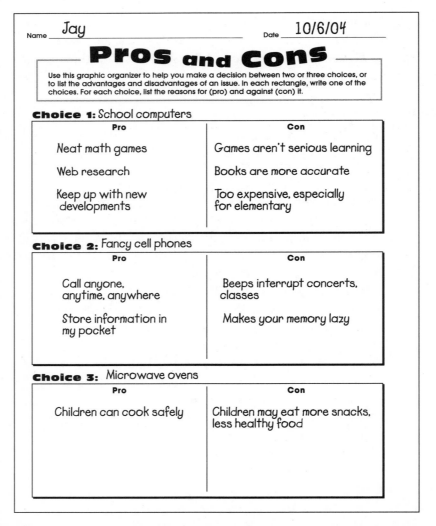

After students have shared some of their ideas with their groups, have them work individually on writing their draft. Remind them to pay particular attention to the standards criteria.

Chapter 5

Reproducible

Prewriting Frameworks

69

Acrostic

Write the assignment topic as one or two nouns and a verb. List the letters of each word in the boxes below. Use those letters to begin words or phrases that relate to the topic.

TOPIC: _____

Highlight your best ideas. Number them in the order in which you will use them in your writing.

Brainstorm

Write your topic in the burst at right.

List anything that comes to your mind about the topic.

_____

_____

_____

Zzz... STOP! Cue yourself: Who? Where? When?

_____

_____

_____

Zzz... STOP! Cue yourself: What could you see? Hear? Taste? Smell?

_____

_____

_____

Zzz... STOP! Cue yourself: How big? What shape? What use?

_____

_____

_____

Zzz... STOP! If you share with other students, hitchhike on their ideas.

_____

_____

_____

Zzz... STOP! Highlight your best ideas. Number them in the order in which you will use them in your writing, or use different colors to circle ideas that belong together.

Name _____ Date _____

Categorize

Write the main topic in the top box. Think: What are some important parts or sections of the topic? Write each part in each box. For each part, write one or two questions to answer while writing.

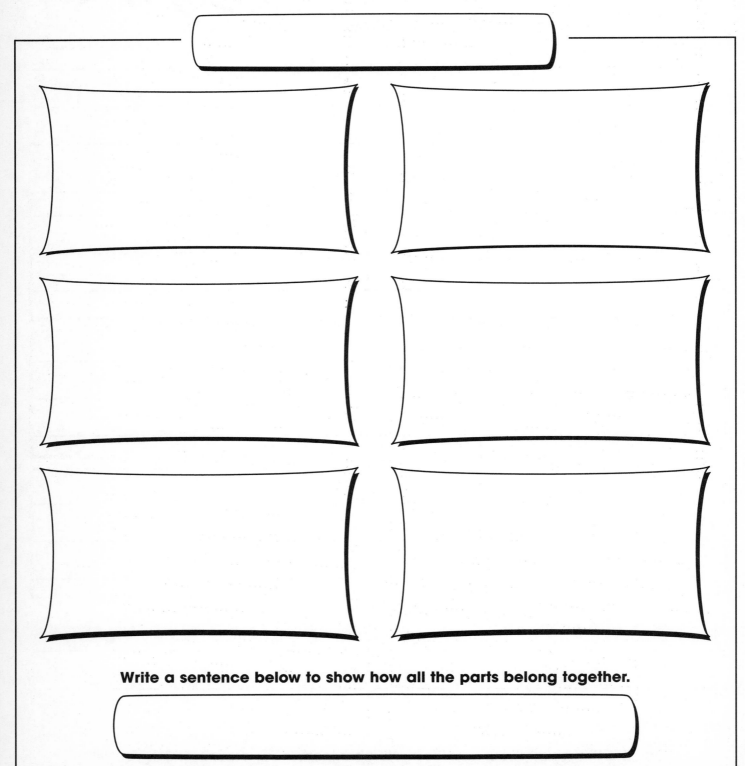

Write a sentence below to show how all the parts belong together.

Cause and Effect

Some processes or events can be explained using cause and effect. Think about the effect and write it in the oval below. Think: What happened to cause that effect? Write a cause in each rectangle. Connect causes and effect with arrows to show if it was a sequence of causes happening one after the other or if the causes happened almost at the same time. In the triangle, write your summary sentence putting all the causes and effects together.

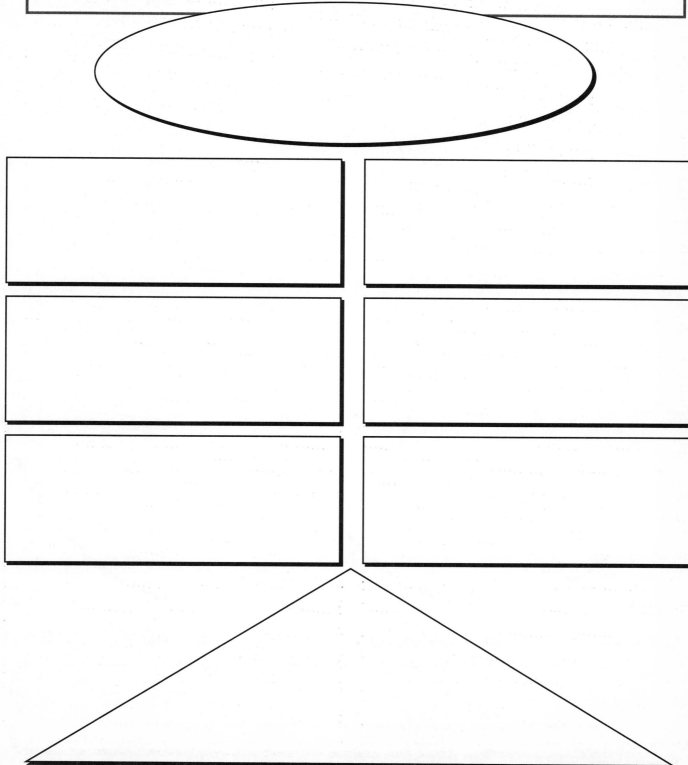

Name _____   Date _____

Compare and Contrast 1

A Venn diagram helps you see how two things are the same and different. Write the name of each item at the top of each ovals. In each oval, draw or write what makes each item unique or different from the other. Where the two ovals overlap, draw or write how the two items are the same.

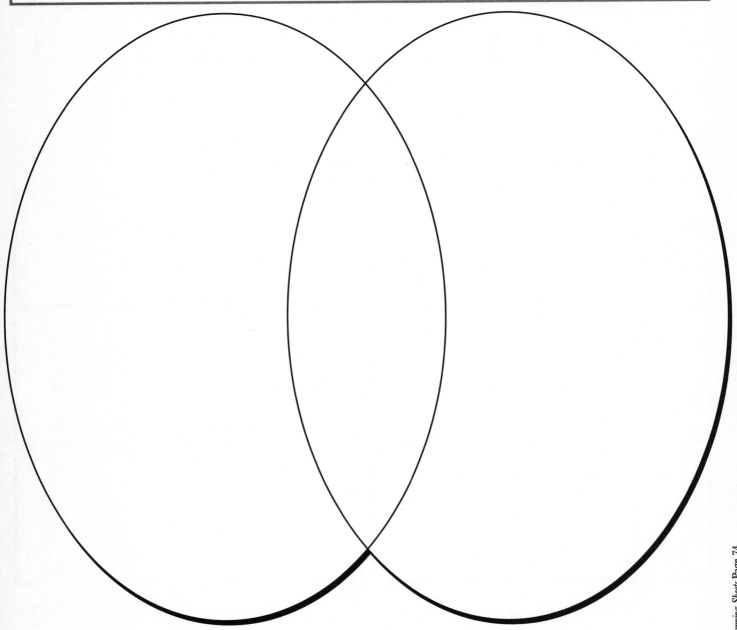

Write a summary sentence below, saying how the items are more alike or more different.

Name _____ Date _____

Compare and Contrast 2

Asking key questions is an effective way to find similarities and differences between two things. At the top of columns 2 and 4, write the names of the two items you are comparing. In the first column, write a question on each row. Answer the questions for each item, noting the unique characteristics (differences) in columns 2 and 4. Note the ways in which the two things are similar in column 3.

Questions	Item 1 (differences)	Both items (similarities)	Item 2 (differences)

Context Analysis

This planning sheet is useful for elaborating on a science or social studies topic. Write the topic here. Then answer each question below.

TOPIC: _____

1. What are its characteristics? What is it like?

_____

_____

_____

2. How has it changed over time?

_____

_____

_____

3. How is it a part of something else?

_____

_____

_____

4. How does it influence other things or people?

_____

_____

_____

5. Why is it important?

_____

_____

_____

Draw

Start by drawing a character in a critical situation in the center panel. Write a speech bubble for the character or a sentence describing the character's difficulty. In the first panel, draw what caused or led to the difficulty, then write a sentence or speech bubble. In the last panel, draw how the character resolves the difficulty. Write a speech bubble or sentence.

Beginning

Middle

End

_____

_____

_____

_____

Imaging

Write the topic in the center box and draw a symbol or sketch to represent the topic.
Think: What do you know about the topic? How do you feel about it? What does it remind you of? Does it fit with a particular time or place? Why is it important? Close your eyes and picture the answers in your mind. As you think of answers, draw symbols, shapes, blocks of color, or sketches, or write single words in the spaces around the central topic. Then use the most powerful image to begin your writing.

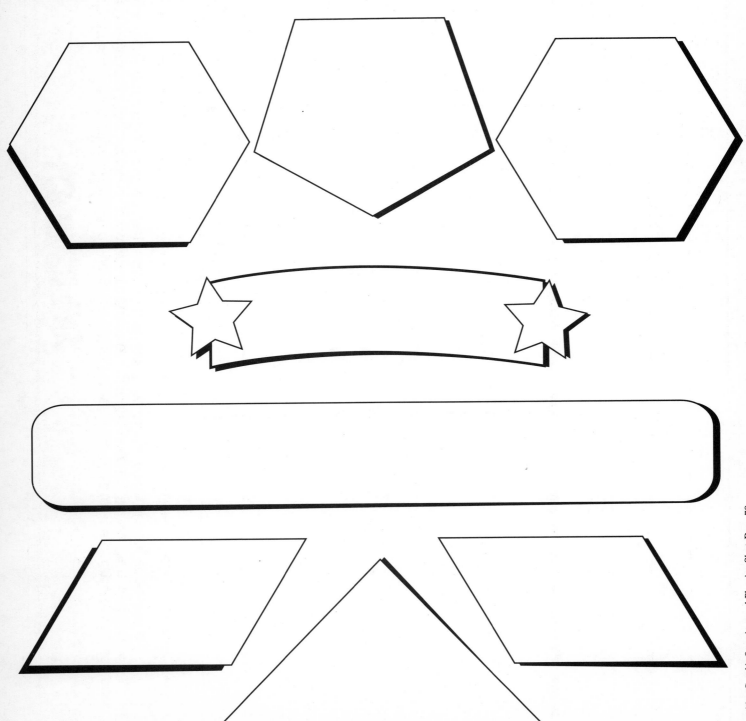

Interview

An interview can help you get information from an expert or eyewitness that you cannot get from a book. Use this planning sheet to think about questions you want to ask.

TOPIC: _____

List at least 3 things you already know about the topic:

Ask these quick questions to get background information:

Who?

Where?

What?

Why?

How?

Write other questions to find out more interesting details:

Narrow down your questions to the 5 most important ones:

Add one question that gives the expert a chance to tell something he/she thinks is especially interesting about the topic:

Write your best questions on a separate piece of paper. Leave some space (at least three lines) between questions for the answers.

Key Words

Write the topic below. In the first column, list nouns that relate to the topic. List verbs in the second column. Share your list with a partner, then with a small group. Add to your lists. Are there words that show movement, action, or feelings? Are there words that help to explain?

TOPIC: _____

Nouns (naming words)	Verbs (action words)

Highlight 5 strong nouns and 5 vivid verbs. Briefly write about the topic below, using at least three nouns and three verbs.

_____

_____

_____

_____

Key Words Extended

Write the topic below. List adjectives, nouns, verbs, and adverbs that relate to the topic. Share your list with a partner, then with a small group. Add to your lists. Are there words that show movement, action, or feelings? Are there words that help to explain?

TOPIC: _____

Adjectives	Nouns	Verbs	Adverbs

Highlight at least two words in each column. Briefly write about the topic below using some of the words you highlighted.

_____

_____

_____

Linking Questions

Write the topic below and answer the questions in the boxes. Use the "How" and "Why" boxes to explain your responses in the "What" box. In the "What" box, number the events in order of importance. At the bottom of the page, write a topic sentence based on your responses.

TOPIC: _____

1. When?

2. Where?

3. Who?

4. What?

5. How?

6. Why?

_____

_____

_____

_____

Make Notes

Write the topic below. Make a few quick notes of facts or subheadings suggested by your notes and the assignment prompt.

TOPIC: _____

- • _____
- • _____
- • _____
- • _____
- • _____
- • _____
- • _____
- • _____
- • _____
- • _____

ORGANIZATION (Look at one or two reference books on the topic. List more categories or subheadings.)

1. _____
2. _____
3 _____
4. _____
5. _____
6. _____
7. _____
8. _____

Choose the subheadings that make most sense to you. These will be sections or chapters of your work. Highlight these subheadings. Copy them onto 5 x 8 cards, one subheading to a card. Jot your notes on the cards. Remember: Your notes should be more like lists of words or phrases, not sentences in a paragraph. Use your own words.

Name _____   Date _____

Outline

Write the main topic below. Break the topic into subtopics (numbers), all of which have the same level of importance. Break each subtopic into sections (letters), also with the same level of importance, and each section into subsections (lowercase Roman numerals). You decide how best to outline your topic.

TOPIC: _____

1. _____

    a. _____

        i. _____

        ii. _____

    b. _____

        i. _____

        ii. _____

    c. _____

        i. _____

        ii. _____

2. _____

    a. _____

        i. _____

        ii. _____

    b. _____

        i. _____

        ii. _____

    c. _____

        i. _____

        ii. _____

3. _____

    a. _____

        i. _____

        ii. _____

    b. _____

        i. _____

        ii. _____

    c. _____

        i. _____

        ii. _____

Paraphrase

Use this framework to make sure you understand the assignment. Every piece of writing needs to fulfill the five domains:

Focus tells what it is about, what its purpose is, and who its audience is.

Content makes the topic interesting with examples and details.

Organization includes a clear beginning, middle, and end, grouping ideas in a sensible way.

Style makes sure the kind of writing fits the audience and the topic, using clear word pictures, strong vocabulary, and varied sentences.

Conventions include correct spelling, punctuation, word use, and paragraphing.

Read your assigned writing prompt. For each domain, write in your own words what you have to do. If the prompt does not explain a domain, make a sensible guess.

Focus: _____

Content: _____

Organization: _____

Style: _____

Conventions: _____

Write below what you have to do to complete the assignment. Pretend that you are explaining it to a friend.

_____

_____

_____

_____

Which prewriting framework is best for this assignment?

_____

PROS and CONS

Use this graphic organizer to help you make a decision between two or three choices, or to list the advantages and disadvantages of an issue. In each rectangle, write one of the choices. For each choice, list the reasons for (pro) and against (con) it.

Choice 1:

Pro	Con

Choice 2:

Pro	Con

Choice 3:

Pro	Con

Questioning

Use this planning sheet to research a social studies or science topic, or to help you summarize a story. You will need a book and small sticky notes. Use the following code:

V = vocabulary (What does this word mean?)
R = reason (Why?)
S = sequence (What happened in what order?)
N = next (What will happen next?)
P = person (Who is this person? What is he/she doing? What is important about him/her?)
I = idea (What is the important idea?)

Read one page or section of the book at a time. If you see something you do not understand or something that is a surprise or puzzle, place a sticky note next to it and label it using the above code. When you have finished with the page or section, go back to your coded sticky notes. Read around each sticky note to find the answer to your question. Choose your three most important questions and answers (if you know them) and write them below. Leave the notes on the page. Repeat with the next page until you finish the whole assignment. If you answered most of your questions, use your notes to start writing. If you still need answers to several questions, ask for help.

_____

_____

_____

_____

_____

_____

_____

_____

_____

_____

_____

_____

_____

_____

_____

Name _____   Date _____

Recall

Use this framework to review what you already know about a topic. After you have jotted down notes in the first five boxes, read the assignment again. Think about the focus, the type of writing, and how you might organize your ideas. Highlight your best ideas and number them in the order you will use for your paragraphs. In the last box, write your introductory sentence.

TOPIC: _____

Personal experience

Things I have read

TV or movies

What other people think

Ideas or words associated with this

Sentence that captures the topic

Role-Play

Acting out a story or event in history can help you gain a better understanding of what happened. You can then write about it in a play or narrative. Before you begin to act it out, make some notes.

TOPIC: _____

Setting: Time _____   Place _____

Main Characters (names and brief descriptions, including what each character wants—motive)

_____

_____

_____

_____

_____

Problem or Special Situation

_____

_____

Notes (Think about what each character wants, how he/she feels about the other characters, and the most important action he/she takes.)

_____

_____

_____

_____

_____

_____

_____

Name _____   Date _____

Sketch and Label

Draw a rough diagram, map, or picture of the object or process to illustrate the assigned topic. Label important parts or steps. Note the function (job) or purpose of each labeled part. Number the parts or steps in the order in which you will write about them. Write an introductory or topic sentence to introduce the assignment.

Story Map

Use this graphic organizer to summarize a story that you have read or plan a story that you will write.

Title: _____

Author: _____

Setting (time)

Setting (place)

Main character

Other important characters

Problem _____

_____

Beginning

Middle

End

What is the message or lesson in the story?

_____

_____

Name _____ Date _____

Think

Read the assignment prompt. Answer the questions below to help you get started with your writing. (Be prepared to go back and revise later.)

TOPIC: _____

Do you understand the focus, content, how it might be organized, purpose, and style to use?	**What do you know about the topic?**
What do you feel about it? What feelings could you bring into the writing?	**Do you have an opinion about it?**
What do you see in your mind?	**What can you say to capture your reader's attention at the beginning?**

Time Line

A time line is useful for planning a biography or history assignment. At the top and bottom of the line, write the beginning and ending dates of the life or time period. On the left side of the time line, list important dates in chronological order next to the cross lines. Write the name of each important event. On the right side of the time line, jot down notes about each event— what happened and why it was important. When you are ready to write, use the dates on the left side to organize the sequence of your writing. Use your notes to help fill out the content.

Web/Cluster

Write the topic in the center box. Think about people, places, and events related to the topic. Write one idea in each of the ovals. Use arrows to join groups of ovals that belong together. Add more ovals if necessary. Write numbers to show the order in which you will write about the groups of ovals.

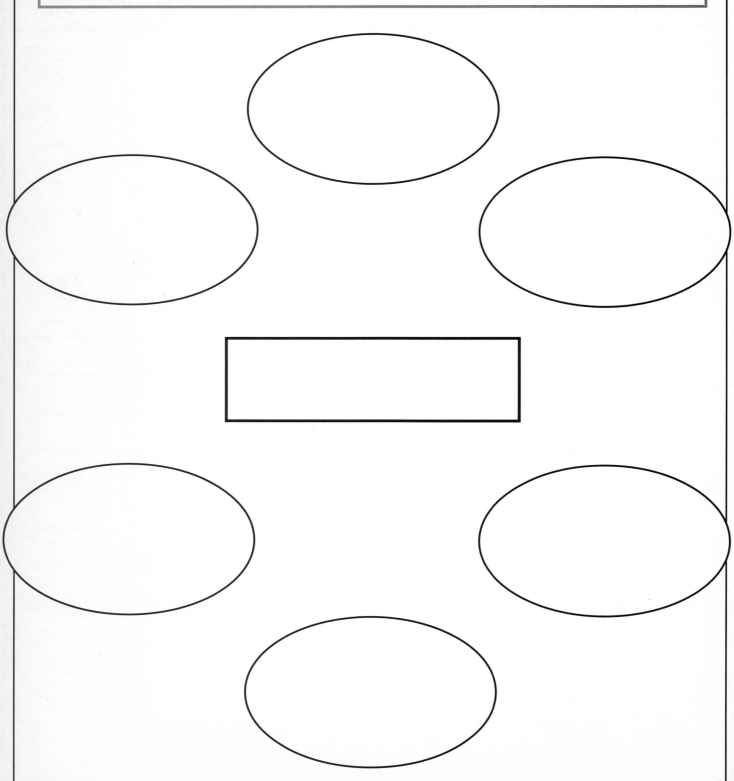

Write Freely

Think about your writing assignment for 30 seconds, then begin writing freely about whatever comes to mind—single words, sentences, ideas, your feelings about having to do this. After five minutes, stop. Read what you wrote. Read the assignment again. Highlight valuable ideas or words. Reconsider. List at least three important ideas that will help you organize your writing. Decide on a point of view. Begin writing the assignment.

_____

_____

_____

_____

_____

_____

_____

_____

_____

_____

_____

_____

_____

_____

_____

1._____

2._____

3._____

References

Calkins, Lucy McCormick. *The Art of Teaching Writing*.
Portsmouth, NH: Heinemann, 1986.

Cotton, Kathleen. *Teaching Composition: Research on Effective Practice*.
Portland, OR: Northwest Regional Education Laboratory, 1988.

Hull, Glynda Ann. "Research on Writing: Building a Cognitive and Social Understanding of Composing." *Toward the Thinking Curriculum: Current Cognitive Research*.
Arlington, VA: Association of Supervision and Curriculum Development, 1989.

Keene, Ellin Oliver, and **Susan Zimmermann**. *Mosaic of Thought: Teaching Comprehension in a Reader's Workshop*. Portsmouth, NH: Heinemann, 1997.

Perl, Sondra. "The Composing Process of Unskilled College Writers."
Research in the Teaching of English, 13(4) (1979): 317–336.

Pritchard, Florence Fay. *Teaching Writing as Thinking*.
Berlin, MD: Shore Educational Associates, 1994.